Eros and
Power

Eros and Power · The Promise of Feminist Theory

Haunani-Kay Trask

upp

University of Pennsylvania Press · Philadelphia

Library of Congress Cataloging-in-Publication Data

Trask, Haunani-Kay.
  Eros and power.

  Bibliography: p.
  Includes index.
  1. Feminism.   2. Patriarchy.   3. Sex role.
4. Civilization.   I. Title.
HQ1154.T66   1986   305.4′2   85-29427
ISBN 0-8122-8007-5 (alk. paper)
ISBN 0-8122-1219-3 (pbk.: alk. paper)

Printed in the United States of America

For Mililani, my beautiful sister

Contents

Preface

For most, if not all, women, the reality of subjugation to men and male-dominated institutions and ideologies has been like the air women breathe or the earth they walk on—a given of the *female* human condition. The values and tasks, behaviors and privileges of men have taken precedence over those of women. Whatever men think has been valued more than what women have thought; whatever men do and say has been valued more than what women have done and said. This is what a "man's world" has meant and continues to mean for men and for women subordinated to them.

Those women throughout history—and there have been many more than we know—who have protested this condition or who have tried to change it have come into their struggles from the culture of their everyday lives, that is, from their experiences as mothers, daughters, sisters, wives, and lovers and as erotic/reproductive objects of men and male society.

My purpose is both to define the fundamentals of the Western system of male dominance which I call, along with other feminists, patriarchy, and to present my own interpretation of the feminist alternative to patriarchy based on selected feminist writings from the American Women's Movement. I am concerned to present patriarchy and one contemporary form of its feminist negation from within the radical, not liberal, feminist tradition, using the language and the interdisciplinary approach characteristic of feminist theory. My analysis is very much a modern view of a modern phenomenon, a radical analysis of a radical, Utopian vision.

Having said this, let me also say that radical feminist theory, from a more traditional point of view, can be seen as part of the dialogue within social theory which seeks to explain the sources and dynamics of Western civilization. In this century, there are two major intellectual perspectives from which these questions are addressed. One is psychological, dealing with individual psychosexual development within the family as a basic

x

explanation for the structure of Western civilization. This analysis proceeds from Freud. Another interpretation focuses on historical development—economic modes, technological evolution, political and class conflict—as the collective forces that structure civilization. This perspective is often labeled Marxist, although it need not be.

Feminist theorists have tended to incorporate insights from both the Marxist and the Freudian traditions in their search for a feminist methodology. But feminists have also argued the centrality of women's experiences in this methodology. That is to say, radical feminists argue for a privileged consciousness that arises from their social practice. In this consciousness, insight and understanding flow from a union of the analytic and the emotional, not from an isolated scientific method which eschews subjectivity and experience as the basis of comprehension. Indeed, it is my argument that feminist insight—from psychology, anthropology, sociology, and above all from poetic expressions—contains a large analysis of Western culture as well as a creative response to it.

My position is that there is a common ground of radical feminism which begins as a serious critique of patriarchy. Simultaneous with critical analyses of society, the corpus of feminist work points to a multidimensional, alternative vision. Whether examining the family, love in its many forms, or the burdens of mothering, all feminists write from a deep sense for a qualitatively better mode of being and living.

This mode I have named the feminist Eros, meaning the feminist formulation of the "life force." With the aid of Herbert Marcuse, I argue that this vision is evidence of a critical consciousness which arises out of women's particular form of social practice: their erotic/reproductive roles of biological and emotional mothering of children, men, and other women. Further, I argue, it is this critical consciousness which enables women to bring a unique analysis to the system of male dominance and to imagine a future world without the oppression of women.

Specifically, I argue that women's oppression is the key to understanding what I call, after Adrienne Rich, the "sexual understructure" of social and political forms, the basic fundamental of Western patriarchy. My argument that the "sexual understructure" is the institutional base of patriarchy is the first cornerstone of my larger theory of the feminist Eros. The radical feminist call for a reorganization of parenting, the family, and our sexual institutions cannot be understood unless

the "sexual understructure" is seen as the source of women's oppression, the grounding of male power over women.

As an alternative vision, the feminist Eros is a challenge to
patriarchal power, the quintessential power of men over women.
I argue that this version of feminist power is explicitly beneficent, taking as its model the nurturing power of the mother, of
her "active gentleness." There is inherent in this formulation
a dual rejection of status and power based in hierarchy and of
relationship founded in psychic, economic, and biologic dependency. There is an emphasis in the feminist Eros on the exchange and sharing of authority, on the equality of the self
among the equality of others.

Because they value communal, social strength, radical feminists have recast the patriarchal meaning of power. They speak
in the language of life: words like "caring" and "need" guide
their discussions against a patriarchal language of "force"
and "will." For the individual, this points to a renunciation
of strength as singular and power as possessive. In the social
realm, compassion and reciprocity are esteemed above manipulation and domination.

Finally, I contend that the feminist Eros projects a metaphor
of the "life force" developed out of the culture of women's everyday lives: the texture and substance of women's reality as mothers, wives, and sexual object/victims. In this context, the new
Eros speaks to a release and refashioning of the life instincts
from the vantage point of women's essential experiences. The
emphasis is on physical and emotional gratifications that connect "life" and "work"; fluid forms and concepts of intimacy
that extend far beyond the merely genital; and integrated social
projects intended to free society from divisive competition and
relentless repression. In the feminist consciousness, Eros as the
totality of the life impulses signifies a release from patriarchal
bondage. Freedom then becomes an integration of our several
selves, a healing of the separation of life from work, sensitivity
from self-consciousness.

Part One of this volume addresses the form and ideology of
male power, showing how this form has historically evolved to
its present state and what the experience of its force has meant
for women. Part Two is an exploration of some of the work of
representative feminists who speak about the feminist Eros in
terms of twin journeys, what I have named the "return to the
mother" and the "return to the body." It is through such journeys that these feminists envision their freedom.

xi

Acknowledgments

There have been many people who brought me to consciousness and nurtured me during the feminist journey that became this book. I wish to acknowledge their *aloha* and *kōkua*.

From my native land, Hawai'i—my father, Bernard Kauka'ohu Trask, who gave me a fighting spirit and a Hawaiian soul and who, if he were alive today, would feel enormously proud of my achievements; my mother, Haunani Cooper Trask, who gave me life; my *'ohana*, especially Mililani, Damien, Paul, and Michael; my dearest friend from small-kid time, Pi'ikea Miyamoto, who was going to drink a bottle of wine for every chapter; my sister, Annette Mente, who listened and cared greatly; my Indian sister, Teresa Mansson, who has given love and sustenance and delicious Indian food; my role model from early years, Alma Ka'iama Cooper; my supporter and *hānai* mother, Mokihana Cockett Aluli; my friend and supporter, Kekuni Blaisdell; my mentor in the study of Hawaiian land tenure, Marion Anderson Kelly; my sister in struggle against racism in Hawai'i, Marilyn Harman; my sister who gave me Hōlualoa, Pat Godfrey; my sister in struggle against U.S. militarism in Hawai'i, Cynthia Thielen; my brother Emmett Aluli, who helped me get back to Madison and who gave me Kalua'aha; and my brothers Bo Kahui and Soli Niheu, who were always there. Also, a special *mahalo nui* to my support committee of students, faculty, and community people who fought against the forces of racism and reaction in the Department of American Studies to get me hired at the University of Hawai'i at Mānoa. For his chairing of this committee and for his steadfast support all these years, I am indebted to Steve Boggs. I also wish to thank Floyd Matson, Franklin Odo, and Jay Gurian for their continuous support, good humor, and sense of justice. They are men of honor. To my dear friend Ed Greevy, photographer extraordinaire, fellow activist, and longtime supporter of the Hawaiian people, my sincere gratitude. And finally, to my native sisters who struggle against American colonialism for an independent Hawai'i, my deep *aloha*.

xiv

From America, professors Ruth Bleier, Joan Roberts, and Elaine Reuben, who began the liberation of my mind from its patriarchal shackles when I was a first-year graduate student at the University of Wisconsin at Madison; my dear friends and fellow students who went through the grind with me in Madison—Ellen Foley, Tom Hamilton, Diane Waldman, George Kundanis, and Janet Spector; and finally, those feminists who inspired me only through their writing and living and whom I never had the joy of meeting—Simone de Beauvoir, Angela Davis, Adrienne Rich, Tillie Olsen, Toni Morrison, Elizabeth Fisher, Catharine MacKinnon, and before them, Emma Goldman and Sappho of Lesbos.

I also wish to acknowledge my teachers. Patrick Riley was delightful and gentle during a time when most others were cold and stodgy.

Booth Fowler deserves unique thanks for seeing me through the disturbing patriarchy that was the Political Science Department of the University of Wisconsin at Madison. He defended my venture into feminist theory back in 1975 when the majority of the department voted against the dissertation topic that became this book. Along with another teacher, Joel Grossman, he was convinced early in my graduate career that I would help him and others to understand the profound contributions of feminism.

I wish to thank Kathy Ferguson and Carroll Smith-Rosenberg for their careful criticism. My argument has benefited from their suggestions.

There have also been those who inspired me since the completion of this book but whose intellectual and personal support were nonetheless integral to its final publication. I would like to acknowledge the remarkable historical works of Richard and Anna Maria Drinnon and, beyond that, the wonderful relationship they share in work and in love. They have been models, and dear friends.

Finally, in every transformation, there are long, dark passages when vision blurs and the heart weakens. During these despairing times, I was cared for and encouraged by David Stannard, *kāne i ka 'ili*. For him, an enduring love:

E maka 'ālohilohi,
Ola na 'ilima wai'ole i ke ao 'ōpua

Haunani-Kay Trask
Waimānalo, Hawai'i

Part One · Male Power

Introduction

It is through a radical exploration of women's hidden body—the body of flesh and feeling, the body of insight and imagination, the body of material and symbolic reality—that contemporary feminists have come to define the causes of women's subordination to men. In the eloquent brevity of Adrienne Rich, female oppression is grounded in

> ... the *sexual understructure* of social and political forms ... a familial-social, ideological, political system in which men,—by force, direct pressure, or through ritual, tradition, law and language, customs, etiquette, education, and the division of labor determine what part women shall or shall not play, and in which the female is everywhere subsumed under the male.[1]

Crucial to Rich's understanding is the notion of an inclusive system of power founded in the primacy of men, as a group, over women, as a group. This system has been called patriarchy. But here, patriarchy does not signify merely the power of the father, as in Freud's symbolic anthropology or in recent feminist works. Rather, patriarchy conveys the power of an entire sex-based class, men, over another sex-based class, women. And it is sexuality and sexual institutions, as Catharine MacKinnon has noted, that are the "primary social sphere" of male power.[2]

Such a sense of patriarchy allows for matrilineal and patrilineal descent, for differences in economic and technological development, for changing ideals, symbols, and myths regarding women. There is, in other words, the conception of "nature, law, the family, and roles as consequences not foundations" of women's subordinated state. The essential characteristic is the pervasive power of men over women's sexuality.[3]

Establishing the presence of the patriarchal order is not difficult. Women may live, work, and achieve in better or worse conditions, in agricultural or industrial societies, under state socialism or bourgeois democracy, but they are always secondary to men.[4] Anthropologist Michele Rosaldo has written:

> Women may be important, powerful, and influential, but . . .
> relative to men of their age and social status, women every-
> where lack generally recognized and culturally valued
> authority. . . . Everywhere men have some *authority* over
> women . . . they have a culturally legitimated right to her
> subordination and compliance.[5]

3

Many feminists argue that woman's status, her inferior position in a given culture, is of man's doing. Thus, during pre-
historic times, when woman's fecundity was openly feared and
misapprehended, men controlled women with strict menstrual
and birth taboos yet venerated the female image as Earth and
Moon Goddess.[6] Later, man's discovery of patrimony, of his contribution to the magical act of creation, doomed woman to the
status of property.[7] Because of her reproductive ability, woman
became an extension of man's being and his fragile quest for immortality. Simone de Beauvoir has argued:

> [Woman's] . . . history in large part is involved with that of
> the patrimony. It is easy to grasp the fundamental importance
> of this institution if one keeps in mind the fact that the owner
> transfers, alienates his existence into his property; he cares
> more for it than for his very life; it overflows the narrow lim-
> its of this mortal lifetime, and continues to exist beyond the
> body's dissolution—the earthly and material incorporation of
> the immortal soul. But this survival can only come about if
> the property remains in the hands of its owner: it can be his
> beyond death only if it belongs to individuals in whom he
> sees himself projected, who are *his*.[8]

As patriarchal property (chattel, gift, dependent, minor),
women have made their lives under varying forms of subjugation in the West: slavery during biblical times, commodity
status in Athenian Greece but comparative equality in Sparta;
absolute legal and economic dependency in the Middle Ages;
increasing personal and civil freedoms with a shift to more psychological forms of oppression in postindustrial society.[9]

In assessing women's heritage of subordination in the West,
feminists have noted historical variations.[10] At different times,
in different places, women have lived their lives under enormously varied circumstances. In certain societies, women have
had major economic power.[11] In other cultures, women's influence and authority have approached equality with men.[12] And in
societies of the advanced industrial West, women's subjugation
to men and to patriarchal values has been softened by the comforts of consumerism, romantic love, and social mobility.

But the constant observation, despite occasional dissenting voices, is women's secondary position relative to men, and beyond this, the predominance of values and institutions crafted by men. It appears to feminists that the rule of men is coextensive with Western culture. That is, Western civilization as we know it has been patriarchal, even while women's energies and achievements have been the bonding elements which enable human society to exist and flourish.[13]

For feminists, this has meant that women have existed within a social and symbolic system where their own needs are suppressed or expressed according to the current design of male supremacy. Adrienne Rich writes:

> Under patriarchy . . . whatever my status or situation, my derived economic class, or my sexual preference, I live under the power of the fathers, and I have access only to so much of privilege or influence as the patriarchy is willing to accede to me, and only for so long as I will pay the price for male approval.[14]

Evidence from anthropology confirms Rich's personal sense. Social authority, according to Claude Lévi-Strauss, has always belonged to men; they must retain structural control over that which they individually own.[15] De Beauvoir's existential rendering of the "imperialism" of the masculine consciousness offers one explanation of male dominance, while our cultural histories—psychological, intellectual, moral—reveal the imprint of patriarchal beliefs, of the oppressive *logos* of the masculine mind: manipulative, aggressive, divided, and distanced from body, materiality, and feeling.[16]

I would argue that this *logos* is but an elaboration of the logic of domination, the will to *power over nature* which informs Western civilization and which, in feminist terms, inscribes patriarchal consciousness. Within the Western ontology, life and being are conceived as a perpetual struggle for power over human and physical nature. With the collective pursuit of the struggle for existence, the basis of culture is transformed from a struggle for pleasure (i.e., satisfaction of the instincts) into a struggle for domination. Herbert Marcuse has elaborated on this analysis:

> The ego which undertook the rational transformation of the human and natural environment revealed itself as an essentially aggressive, offensive subject, whose thoughts and ac-

4

tions were designed for mastering objects. It was a subject *against* an object. . . . Nature (its own as well as the external world) were "given" to the ego as something that had to be fought, conquered, and even violated—such was the precondition for self-preservation and self-development.

The struggle begins with the perpetual internal conquest of the "lower" faculties of the individual: his sensuous and appetitive faculties. . . . The struggle culminates in the conquest of external nature, which must be perpetually attacked, curbed, and exploited in order to yield to human needs. . . . Nature is *a priori* experienced by an organism bent to domination and therefore experienced as susceptible to mastery and control.[17]

According to Marcuse, successful repression (basic modification of the instincts) and aggression (against the environment) enable Western civilization. But the aggressive ego which is formed from this necessity creates and reproduces the logic of domination. What originally was a struggle for pleasure is transformed into a struggle for security, organized in the interest of domination (surplus-repression).

Ananke (scarcity) is experienced as the barrier against the satisfaction of the life instincts, which seek pleasure, not security. And the "struggle for existence" is originally a struggle for pleasure: culture begins with collective implementation of this aim. Later, however, the struggle for existence is organized in the interest of domination: the erotic basis of culture is transformed. When philosophy conceives of the essence of being as Logos, it is already the Logos of domination—commanding, mastering, directing reason, to which man and nature are to be subjected.[18]

Phylogenetically, the logos of domination which Marcuse identified as the Western essence of being begins with the history of man as the history of repression. Following Freud, Marcuse accepts a basic description of human evolution: (1) Western culture constrains the instinctual structure of the individual; (2) such constraint is the precondition for progress; (3) instincts must be deflected from their goal, inhibited in their aim, because they strive for gratification as an end in itself. Thus, according to Marcuse, "civilization begins when the primary objective—namely, integral satisfaction of needs—is effectively renounced."[19]

The striving for gratification is Freud's *pleasure principle*. It

5

is transformed under the impact of scarcity, of environmental constraint—the *reality principle*. This transformation first occurs during the primary love relationship with the mother, whose significance cannot be underestimated. "The replacement of the pleasure principle by the reality principle is the great traumatic event in the development of man."[20]

Temporarily leaving aside the early role of the mother, it is central to the feminist concept of patriarchy, as Western civilization's "sexual understructure," that the reality principle be understood as the product of social organization. The ascendance of the reality principle

> is not unique but recurs throughout the history of mankind and of every individual. Phylogenetically, it occurs first in the *primal horde*, when the *primal father* monopolizes power and pleasure and enforces renunciation on the part of the sons. Ontogenetically, it occurs during the period of early childhood, and submission to the reality principle is enforced by the parents and other educators. But, both on the generic and the individual level, submission is continuously reproduced.
>
> The reality principle materializes in a system of institutions. And the individual, growing up within such a system, learns the requirements of the reality principle as those of law and order, and transmits them to the next generation.[21]

The pleasure principle is never wholly defeated, and reappears in phantasy and the return of the repressed. Although a social product, the organization of repression is supported by repression from within. There is a constant war between the pleasure principle (absence from repression—freedom) and the reality principle (repression—domination). The id battles the superego, the unconscious threatens the conscious. Between the two impulses is the ego, created by pressures from the external world yet continually striving for gratification, like the id, but in a modified, delayed form.

The formation of the individual—id-ego-superego—and the concepts of the unconscious and infantile sexuality depend on Freud's theory of the instincts. Emphasizing the common origin of the instincts, Freud first identified two primary forces—the sexual and the self-preservative. Later, this division evolved into the Life (Eros) instincts and the Death (Thanatos) instincts. The instincts are plastic, subject to the organization of the reality principle and therefore susceptible to modification; the struggle between them constitutes the primary dynamic within the individual.

For Freud, the Life instincts tended toward greater unities, while the Death instincts tended toward inertia, the state of inorganic life. But the common origin of the instincts remained problematic and obscure. With the introduction of the concept of narcissism, Freud's instincts seemed to become derivatives of Eros.

For Marcuse, the discovery of narcissism completely changed the nature of the Death instinct. In a radical redefinition of Thanatos, Marcuse contended in 1955 that the single principle of organic life appeared to be a striving for integral quiescence. Thus the Death instinct was not destructiveness for its own sake, but for the relief of tension. It was "an expression of the eternal struggle against suffering and repression."[22]

Marcuse's revision allowed him several others. He could argue, as Freud could not, for the possibility of nonrepressive sublimation, and therefore a nonrepressive civilization. With his creative additions of the concepts of *surplus-repression* and the *performance principle* (prevailing historical form of the reality principle), Marcuse could make the very persuasive argument that the interests of domination prolonged scarcity by distributing it unequally. Moreover, progress was not incompatible as long as domination continued. At a certain historical point— advanced industrial capitalism—abundance superseded scarcity, unmasking the reality of the *organization of scarcity* in the interests of domination.

In Marcuse's revisions, war, aggression, and repression become the warping results of domination rather than of the civilizing process, as Freud had argued. Since Thanatos is not destructiveness but a yearning for peace, the Death instinct no longer is a preventive to the achievements of nonrepressive civilization. With the elimination of scarcity, the attainment of freedom and happiness (the integral satisfaction of needs) becomes an exciting possibility.

Because of his redefinition of Thanatos, Marcuse could return with new arguments to the organization of the reality principle and its effects on the instincts. He could extrapolate from Freud's theory, creating his own radical theory by separating biological from sociohistorical forms of the instincts. He did this in the following formulation:

SURPLUS-REPRESSION: The restrictions necessitated by social domination. This is distinguished from *(basic) repression*, which is the "modification" of the instincts necessary for the perpetuation of the human race in civilization

PERFORMANCE PRINCIPLE: The prevailing historical form of the reality principle

In looking behind the reality principle, Marcuse saw not the presence of scarcity, as Freud did, but its organization and distribution for the benefit of a few. Western civilization appeared, in the light of sophisticated Marxism, as a history of sexually based domination where individual needs were pressed into the service of others. Marcuse argued:

> . . . the *distribution* of scarcity as well as the effort of overcoming it, the mode of work, have been *imposed* upon individuals—first by mere violence, subsequently by a more rational utilization of power. However, no matter how useful this rationality was for the progress of the whole, it remained the rationality of *domination*, and the gradual conquest of scarcity was inextricably bound up with and shaped by the interest of domination. . . . Domination is exercised by a particular group or individual in order to sustain and enhance itself in a privileged position. Such domination does not exclude technical, material, and intellectual progress, but only as an unavoidable by-product while preserving irrational scarcity, want, and constraint.[23]

While Marcuse acknowledged that *any* form of the reality principle demanded considerable repressive control of the instincts, he argued that specific historical institutions and the specific interests of domination introduced additional controls over and above those necessary for civilized association. These controls constituted surplus-repression.

The relationship between Eros and Thanatos, then, depends on the role of both basic repression and surplus-repression. Marcuse explained:

> The modification of the instincts under the reality principle affects the life instinct as well as the death instinct; but the development of the latter becomes fully understandable only in the light of the development of the life instincts, i.e., of the repressive *organization of sexuality*. The sex instincts bear the brunt of the reality principle.[24]

Like basic repression, surplus-repression begins with the organization of sexuality. However, basic repression is essential to the formation of the ego as it seeks to balance the demands of a driving id with those of an imperfect world. Surplus-repression, on the other hand, is the organization of certain forms of repression specifically for the purposes of domination. For example, surplus-repression is manifested in the subjugation of the sex instincts to genitality and the function of procreation. The gratification of nongenital instincts and nonprocreative genitality are tabooed as perversions. The organization of procreative sexuality is then channeled into monogamic institutions. Among other things, these institutions enforce a limitation on the organism's drive to pleasure. The process of enforcement is a long development through childhood and puberty, during which time the body is progressively desexualized by parents and other authorities. Restrictions on the libido appear rational because they seem universal. Moreover, they operate on the individual as external, objective laws and as an internalized force. The "conscience" of the individual becomes the social (moral) authority: people live their repression freely.

Surplus-repression of the sex instincts brings the organism into line with the demands of an acquisitive, aggressive (patriarchal) society. Monogamy and genitality, for example, prescribe focused heterosexual possession, prohibiting spontaneous liaisons and nongenital sex as *immoral* or *unnatural*. If morality is seen as the repressive "conscience" of the individual, then "perversions" are indeed immoral. They are the return of the repressed, confounding the prescription of sex within marriage for procreation. By their immoral character, perversions defy the demands of an alienating society. They threaten the performance principle at its roots of organization—the sex instincts. Thus the social threat of the perversions rests not so much in their actual transgressions of social mores but in their refusal of social authority itself. This is why, as Freud noted, repression of the instincts is so severe.

The end result of surplus-repression is an alteration of sexuality from an autonomous principle governing the entire organism into a specialized function, a means to an end. This end is a desexualization of the body for the fulfillment of the performance principle, that is, alienated labor.

The transformation of the desiring human organism into an instrument of alienated labor occurs under the rule of the performance principle. Through the distribution of time—the institutionalization of the working day and the consequent structuring of leisure time—the "timeless" pleasure principle is subjugated to the performance principle. This principle decrees an acquisitive, aggressive ego. During the working day, individuals are forced to submit to this mode—hence alienated labor. (Marcuse argues that not all labor needs to be alienating. For him, the irreconcilable conflict is not between work [reality principle] and Eros [pleasure principle] but between alienated labor [performance principle] and Eros).

For both Freud and Marcuse, surplus-repression of the sex instincts weakens Eros, altering the balance between Life and Death. This weakening mutilates both instincts. Thanatos appears as unlimited aggression (no longer as a desire for peace); Eros appears as alienation—the absence of gratification, the negation of the pleasure principle. Phylogenetically, this altered struggle is portrayed through the performance principle: alienated individuals under the rationalized domination of an antagonistic, expanding society.

In accepting this view of Western civilization, I would argue that Marx's analysis focuses on one form of the organization of domination, while Freud's analysis of the patriarchal family focuses on another. But neither of these investigations addresses the organization of women's domination, except tangentially. Even Marcuse, who approaches the problem of women's oppression from the possibility of revolutionary potential, fails to analyze the specific conditions of women's existence, substituting instead an idealized, abstract formulation of female essence.[25]

If the common ground of Marxist, Freudian, and feminist analyses is the existence of Western civilization as domination, their unique perspectives suggest alternative explanations. The failure of the first two modes of analysis to account for women's domination has led feminists to develop another critique of civilization, one which combines elements of Marx and Freud but which goes beyond them by addressing the connection between women's subordination and the organization of human sexuality.

For example, the psychic maiming that both Freud and Marcuse identify as the cost of civilization produces a deformation of the life (Eros) impulses and a domination of the death (Thanatos) instincts. For Freud, the cost is severe but inevitable, even to the recurrence of war. For Marcuse, however, utopian possibilities present themselves in the historical transformation of the reality principle into the performance principle: the heritage of the latter (a mature, technological civilization) sets the preconditions for the liberation of Eros and a triumph over Thanatos.

But the problem for Marcuse is the question of where the political component of the liberation of Eros will arise. His idealization of women's passive, "more human" nature creates contradictions in his argument that they possess revolutionary potential.[26] And his aesthetic critique, while beautiful and convincing, begs the question of praxis.

At this point, feminists suggest a return to the source of instinctual repression: the organization of sexuality within society. Initially, feminists argue, the force of civilization is more than repressive and aggressive. In its conquest of nature, the mastering ego is firstly misogynist, woman-hating. Because she is the ever-desired reality of man's *lower* and more dangerous because more gratifying nature, woman is continually subordinated to man as nature is subordinated to culture. If Western culture is indeed founded in the primary, methodical sublimation of sexuality, then woman, as the very embodiment of sexuality, is at the core of the repressive dialectic of civilization. Thus feminists have added to the discoveries of Freud and Marcuse the insight that the organization of sexuality entails not only the savage repression of Eros, but also the specific displacement of Eros onto women.

An illustration will suggest my meaning. Both Freud and Marcuse identify repression of the sexual instincts as necessary for civilized human association. Marcuse further suggests that additional (surplus) repression is forced on the human impulses in the interests of domination. His particular concern is the surplus repression needed to maintain alienated labor, labor that is demanded by an aggressive society. Building on the analysis of a repression of the body, feminists have argued that women's sexuality has been constructed in such a way as to perpetuate male control over, and definition of, the experience of sexuality. This definition and control has both structural roots and psychological manifestations. Psychologically, for example, women experience their enforced vulnerability as erotically appealing to men.[27] Similarly, the impossible and deforming burden of self-sacrificing love, of emotionally reproducing men, children, and themselves, has been engendered in women as mothering. When supported by the sexual division of labor (private/public), this erotic/reproductive constellation binds women in a psychic and structural way to a painful, oppressive existence. While the desire and capacity to mother (emotionally as well as psychologically) are reproduced in women through exclusive female child-care in the patriarchal family,[28] the ideology and organization of the public world lend structural insurance to women's erotic/reproductive characterization.[29] Whether women enter the *work* world or not, their relational, nurturant capacities, coupled with their erotic potential, continue to form the basis of their cultural value. Men's control over women's bodies—erotic, reproductive, imagistic, symbolic—is the key to women's valuation and their subjugated condition.[30]

In Marcuse's language, this feminist argument identifies women's sexuality and sexually based institutions, particularly women's mothering and the social forms that surround it (e.g., the exchange of women, mandatory heterosexuality), as surplus-repression. These forms of surplus-repression, I will argue, are both building-blocks of Western society as well as the "sexual understructure" of women's oppression. Certainly, these forms serve the interests of men. Finally, the sexual understructure is part of the negation of Eros, and a contributing factor in the increasing power of Thanatos. A reversal of this trend depends not only on the technical level of culture (Marcuse) but also, as feminists argue, on a transformation of our sexual institutions.

Notes

1. Adrienne Rich, *Of Woman Born* (New York: Norton, 1976), pp. 56–57.

2. For a feminist rehabilitation of Freud where patriarchy does signify the power of the father, see Juliet Mitchell, *Psycho-analysis and Feminism* (New York: Vintage Books, 1974). For an early analysis of patriarchy as a system of power, see Kate Millet, *Sexual Politics* (New York: Avon, 1971). For the most recent theoretical formulation of the basis of men's power over women, see Catharine A. MacKinnon, "Feminism, Marxism, Method, and the State: An Agenda for Theory," in *Feminist Theory: A Critique of Ideology*, ed. Nannerl Keohane, Michelle Rosaldo, and Barbara Gelpi (Chicago: University of Chicago Press, 1982), pp. 1–30.

3. MacKinnon, "Feminism, Marxism, Method, and the State," p. 15.

4. For comparative purposes, see Peggy R. Sanday, *Female Power and Male Dominance* (New York: Cambridge University Press, 1981); Esther Boserup, *Woman's Role in Economic Development* (New York: St. Martin's Press, 1970); Margaret Mead, *Sex and Temperament in Three Primitive Societies* (New York: Morrow, 1963), and *Male and Female* (New York: Morrow, 1949); Karen Sacks, *Sisters and Wives: The Past and the Future of Sexual Equal-*

ity (Westport, Conn.: Greenwood Press, 1979); Eleanor Leacock, *Myths of Male Dominance* (New York: Monthly Review Press, 1981); Alice Schlegel, ed., *Sexual Stratification: A Cross-Cultural View* (New York: Columbia University Press, 1977).

5. Michelle Zimbalist Rosaldo, "Woman, Culture and Society: A Theoretical Overview," in *Woman, Culture and Society*, ed. Michelle Rosaldo and Louise Lamphere (Stanford: Stanford University Press, 1974), pp. 17, 21.

6. See, e.g., M. Esther Harding, *Woman's Mysteries: Ancient and Modern* (New York: Harper, 1971); and Erich Neumann, *The Great Mother* (Princeton: Princeton University Press, 1972).

7. See Elizabeth Fisher's brilliant analysis of the connection between the discovery of patrimony, the domestication of animals, and the subjugation of women, in *Woman's Creation: Sexual Evolution and the Shaping of Society* (New York: Anchor Press, 1979), especially Parts IV and V, pp. 177–327.

8. Simone de Beauvoir, *The Second Sex* (New York: Knopf, 1953), p. 75.

9. Ibid., pp. 56–128.

10. See Fisher, *Woman's Creation.*

11. See Boserup, *Woman's Role in Economic Development.*

12. See the many comparative articles in *Woman, Culture and Society*, ed. Rosaldo and Lamphere. Also M. Kay Martin and Barbara Voorhies, *Female of the Species* (New York: Columbia University Press, 1975); and Sanday, *Female Power and Male Dominance.*

13. This is Mitchell's argument based on the observations of Lévi-Strauss. See her *Psycho-analysis and Feminism*, pp. 370–381.

14. Rich, *Of Woman Born*, p. 58.

15. Claude Lévi-Strauss's argument in *The Elementary Structures of Kinship* (Boston: Beacon, 1969).

16. See Mary Daly's critique of Western philosophy and religion in *Beyond God the Father* (Boston: Beacon, 1973).

17. Herbert Marcuse, *Eros and Civilization* (Boston: Beacon, 1966), pp. 109–110.

18. Ibid., p. 125.

19. Ibid., p. 11.

20. Ibid., p. 15.

21. Ibid.

22. Ibid., p. 29.

23. Ibid., pp. 36–37.

24. Ibid., p. 40.

25. See Joan Landes's critique of Marcuse's feminism in "Marcuse's Feminist Dimension" (Paper delivered at the 1978 Annual Meeting of the American Political Science Association, New York, 1978).

26. Ibid., pp. 18–26.

27. See Andrea Dworkin's analysis of women's vulnerability and its erotic attraction for men as seen through a study of pornography in *Pornography: Men Possessing Women* (New York: G. P. Putnam's Sons, 1981). See also Ellen Morgan, *The Erotization of Male Dominance/Female Submission* (Pittsburgh: Know Inc., 1975).

28. This is Nancy Chodorow's argument in her exhaustive psychoanalytic account, *The Reproduction of Mothering: Psychoanalysis and the Sociology of Gender* (Berkeley: University of California Press, 1978). See also Dorothy Dinnerstein's argument in *The Mermaid and the Minotaur* (New York: Harper, 1976).

29. See Millett, *Sexual Politics*.

30. See MacKinnon, "Feminism, Marxism, Method, and the State."

14

One · Ideology and Ontology

As other systems of power, male dominance can be identified by its ideological justifications, ontological assumptions, sociological structures, historical evolution, and psychological formations. Feminists have explored these areas, focusing on the sources and institutions that anchor male power and perpetuate female powerlessness.

Ideology

The association of women with nature stands out as perhaps the most familiar justification of the sexual understructure.[1] While many feminists have noted this and have carefully explicated the multiple connections between nature and women, anthropologist Sherry Ortner has suggested that women's seeming intractable attachment to nature is best understood in the context of other human universals: "Every human being has a physical body and a sense of nonphysical mind, is part of a society of other individuals, and an inheritor of a cultural tradition, and must engage in some relationships, however mediated, with 'nature,' or the nonhuman realm, in order to survive."[2] Stating that every culture (defined as human consciousness and its products) has asserted a distinction between culture and nature, Ortner locates the unique attribute of culture in its capacity to transcend (shape, modify, change) nature. Because of this transcendence, culture is perceived as "superior" to nature.

Ortner has been criticized for universalizing her analysis. As Peggy Sanday has shown, not all cultures view humans as separate and above nature. Nor do all cultures evolve the same male dominant modes. And Carolyn Merchant has argued that even in the West, where culture *is* asserted over nature, science and technology have greatly increased culture's rapacious domain over nature.[3]

If limited to the West, however, Ortner's analysis is helpful, since women *have been* viewed as a more integral part of nature than men. And it is this continuing association with nature (the "naturalization" process) which comprises part of the justification of women's inferior status. Ortner argues that

> . . . if women were considered part of nature, then culture would find it "natural" to subordinate, not to say oppress, them. . . . [W]omen are seen as being *closer* to nature than men. That is, culture (still equated relatively unambiguously with men) recognizes that women are active participants in its special processes, but at the same time sees them as being more rooted in, or having more direct affinity with, nature.[4]

In linking the "naturalization" of women to the larger nature/culture hierarchy, Ortner has lent a persuasive sophistication to her theory. Given Western culture's claimed superiority to nature, the perception of women as more grounded in nature than men will always result in some form of female subordination. But the variety and ambiguity of women's relation to the world is sensitively accounted for in Ortner's analysis of women as "closer to" rather than simply representative of nature.

The distinction is meaningful. Women, like men, are capable of invention and creation, for they also possess human consciousness and contribute to social intercourse and to cultural endeavors. Because of their obvious membership in human society, then, women cannot be wholly relegated to the realm of "nature" or the "natural." Conveniently, women come to occupy an *intermediate position* between nature and culture: more conscious and purposeful than animals, but less creative and transcendent than men. In understanding women as intermediaries, anthropologists have explored women's conscious role in human society, and the pejorative valuation of that role as secondary and "inferior."

Predictably, the association of women with nature begins with the female body and its procreative functions. The "naturalization" process then resonates backward and forward in time, explaining and encompassing women's history, their collective and individual psychologies, and their social roles. Thus, Ortner argues, a basic reproductive fact has cultural significance on at least three levels: (1) woman's body is involved with species life more of the time than man's body, which is relatively free to pursue the projects of culture; (2) woman's reproductive capacity places her in social roles which seem closer to nature and therefore at a lower order of the cultural process than man's social roles; (3) woman's social roles fashion different psychic forma-

16

tions, which are perceived as direct products of a "natural" and therefore secondary process.

Even with the mitigations of the modern age, woman's continuing bondage to the species is without question. Of greater import is the valuation of woman's life-giving capacity in opposition to projects of culture.

For example, Simone de Beauvoir has observed that giving birth, however painful and momentous for woman, remains an animal reality common to all living things. Because of this manifest animality, woman appears, in the patriarchal eye, to be grounded in the natural realm. Man, who does not experience physical reproduction, appears to transcend life through his cultural projects. Consequently, man comes to value invention, symbolization, and action more than the reproduction and repetition of life. This superior valuation separates the animal from the cultural, the repetitive from the creative. Because she is associated with both the animal *and* the repetitive, woman is subordinated to man as nature is subordinated to culture.

But man's attempts to separate and subdue the natural within the cultural can never be entirely successful, for the human being partakes of both. Mind is nonexistent without body; feeling becomes little more than stimulation if consciousness is lacking. Nevertheless, the exacting assertion of culture over nature is reflected in the continuing struggle of men over women. And the structure of women's partial defeat is to be found in their mediating functions.

Woman's intermediate status illuminates her historical dependence on man. Grounded in her reproductive capacities and man's subsequent subordination of her, this dependence is "naturalized" through psychic formations, later socialization, custom, and institutions. Woman becomes a *pretext* rather than an *agent*, an intermediary rather than a sovereign.

For example, women's traditional confinement to the domestic sphere is better understood in light of the naturalization process. From the physiological point of view, the "naturalness" of childbirth gives rise to the "naturalness" of lactation, which gives rise to the "naturalness" of child-care, which in turn gives rise to the "naturalness" of belonging in the domestic realm. But the seeming naturalness of the process also stems from the character of children. Incapacitated, unsocialized, and immature, children are themselves categorized with nature. Consequently, women's identification with nature is compounded by their closeness to children. Further, women's near-universal

17

responsibility has been not only to feed and clean children, but also to socialize them for entry into the adult world, that is, to convert the *natural* (the infant) into the *cultural* (the person).

Other intriguing realities are enlightened by women's "mediating" status. Our mothers may prepare us for the adult world, but it is our fathers who control our entry and lead us into the public realm. The ancient alliance (and threat) of women and the domestic world against men and the public world can be seen as one aspect of the nature/culture paradox. Like women's alleged inferiority itself, the whole nature/culture tension is a conceptual product, and thus mirrors all the variations of the collective human mind. In some Western societies, the domestic/public dichotomy is not as severe, and therefore not as restrictive of women's activities, as in other Western societies where divisions are rigid and subsequent limitations profound. Tellingly, the relative severity of the domestic/public split has been suggested as an index of women's oppression.[5]

The argument that woman's psyche is seen as closer to nature is most controversial since many confuse the analysis of psychic "naturalization" with an apology for its continuance. However, my own view is that the specific sexual psychology of women, as that of men, is set in motion by the dynamics of the patriarchal family, especially female child-care, and is supported by other basic units of the sexual understructure—exclusive gender, mandatory heterosexuality, the sexual division of labor. Understanding women's association with nature is a precondition for analyzing their cultural subordination.

Beginning with relative traits on a masculine-feminine continuum, anthropologists argue that the features of Western family structure—women's responsibility for early child-care and for (at least) later female socialization—tend to create a given "feminine" and "masculine" personality.

> One relevant dimension that does seem pan-culturally applicable is that of relative concreteness vs. relative abstractness: the feminine personality tends to be involved with concrete feelings, things, and people, rather than with abstract entities; it tends toward personalism and particularism. [M]en are more objective and inclined to relate in terms of relatively abstract categories, women more subjective and inclined to relate in terms of relatively concrete phenomena.[6]

This analysis builds on Nancy Chodorow's argument that women's central role in child-care (in psychoanalysis, the "omnipotent mother") results in certain elements within male and female ego structures. The pre-Oedipal period (infant-mother), in which individuation and primary love are paramount, is prolonged for the girl. She is kept closer to her mother, both emotionally and psychologically, for a longer period of time than is the boy. The boy is urged into the Oedipal stage (mother-infant-father) sooner, thereby confronting gender issues and sexuality before the girl. The result, Chodorow contends, is a greater relational capacity in women but a concomitant increase in their need for emotional nurturance. Men, meanwhile, reflect a lesser capacity for relationship (although a strong need for nurturance), and a more independent ego with less flexible boundaries.

In the sociology of adult life, women's greater relational capacity is encouraged by the public/private division which characterizes life, feeling, and domestic duties, particularly childrearing, as female domains. Men's lesser relational capacities are equally supported by the same division, which places them in the world of impersonal work, unfeeling rationality, and public activity. The structural conditions of childrearing thus produce gender differences which ground fundamental relations between men and women: sexual politics.[7]

With the nature/culture analysis, women's mediating functions are seen to provide vital, although devalued, services to human society. In their reproduction and care of children, in their domestic duties, and in their relational approach to the world, women afford culture (men) a temporary, mediated transcendence of nature at serious cost to women's own personal transcendence (autonomy, creativity).

The nature/culture scheme finds supporting corollaries everywhere. In Freud, for example, a closed characterization of the "inferior" feminine personality lends intellectual defense to the cultural prejudice that women are enveloped by their bodies and driven by emotion, materiality, and the vicissitudes of human reproduction. Freud justified women's exploitation (economic dependence on men) and oppression (confinement to domestic duties), through his argument that women's psychology (based in their inferior anatomy) rendered them incapable of intellectual achievement, ethical behavior and stable, authoritative activity in the public realm. In a phrase, Freud "naturalized" women's psychology, and thereby legitimated their cultural subordination. As a result, women are seen as mediators in the civilizing process, while civilization itself remains a male domain.

In the realm of mythology, Simone de Beauvoir has explored

the fascinating history of women's association with nature. With confirmation from the works of Joseph Campbell, H. R. Hays, Jane Harrison, and C. J. Jung, de Beauvoir points to the recurrent portrayal of women as mysterious, dark, and treacherous, or simple, enlightening, and redemptive. Typically, when man feared nature, he feared woman's virginity and bloody menstruation. Often failing to connect intercourse and paternity, man stood in awe of birth and nurturance. But when he conquered nature, he cast woman as his prey. He would possess and penetrate her as he possessed and penetrated the cultivated earth. Like the earth, however, woman was unpredictable. Erotic and desirable, she could also be too carnal and therefore annihilating. Thus, in the agricultural period, after the discovery of metal and cultivation, powerful female gods decline. In their place, come less powerful deities, some evil, some pure, but all subordinated to central male gods.[8]

In the Middle Ages, Christianity begins to degrade and simultaneously spiritualize woman. The church fathers, especially Paul, Augustine, and Jerome, focus their hatred of the flesh on women, thereby establishing the basis for modern Christian "sexual" morality. As the embodiment of threatening sexuality, women are split into "virgin" and "whore," with the wife left an ambiguous if necessary role. The Virgin Mary becomes an intermediary between man and his male god. The Pauline doctrine of the "spiritual body" ascends to heights of virginal purity—the salvation of Mary's asexual mothering. Eve, meanwhile, symbolizes the Augustinian fear of the pleasures and temptations of the flesh.[9] Thus has man, through his various mythic and religious forms, projected his uncertain relationship with woman, and through her with nature. Mythologist Joseph Campbell writes:

> The fear of woman and the mystery of her motherhood have been for the male no less impressive imprinting forces than the fears and mysteries of the world of nature itself. And there may be found in the mythologies and ritual traditions of our entire species innumerable instances of the unrelenting efforts of the male to relate himself effectively—in the way, so to speak, of an antagonistic cooperation—to these two alien yet intimately constraining forces: woman and the world.[10]

Perhaps more than any other artifact, myth illustrates the deep ambiguity toward women inherent in the patriarchal mind. Beyond the sense of a middle position between nature and culture, and the sense of a "mediating" or "conversion" function, woman's intermediacy also implies symbolic ambiguity.

Menstrual pollution serves as a telling example. Far from representing an archaic taboo, menstrual defilement survives as concept and institution in the most "advanced" of countries, including the United States. For example, recent historians of the menstrual taboo argue:

21

> In our culture, specifically twentieth-century America, women continue to suffer the taboos of centuries. Law, medicine, religion, and psychology have isolated and devalued the menstruating woman. Women who experience debilitating mental or physical pain at menstruation . . . are made the prototype for all. Thus, menstruation is a factor in the control of women by men not only in ancient and primitive societies . . . but also in our post-industrial world.[11]

Even in modern times, menstrual blood is seen as both the source of pollution and the promise of conception—simultaneously *sacred* and *accursed*. Thus, while barred from influencing any part of the procurement or processing of food (e.g., hunting, harvesting, cooking, serving, even eating with men), the young woman at menarche has also been deemed ready for marriage and exchange. Taboos of exclusion and contact, especially sexual intercourse, have focused on women's contaminating potential; hence their magical power to endanger men and all of society.[12]

In Western civilization, Judaism and Christianity have forbidden menstrual intercourse because the woman is "unclean." And in Israel, hardly a "primitive" society, the infamous Levitical injunction continues to structure marital laws, religious mores, and sexual behavior to this day.[13] Listen to the Levitical litany:

> And if a woman have an issue, and her issue in her flesh be blood, she shall be put apart seven days: and whosoever toucheth her shall be unclean until the even.
>
> And everything that she lieth upon in her separation shall be unclean: every thing also that she sitteth upon shall be unclean.
>
> And whosoever toucheth her bed shall wash his clothes, and bathe himself in water, and be unclean until the even.
>
> And if any man lie with her at all, and her flowers be upon him, he shall be unclean seven days; and all the bed whereon he lieth shall be unclean.[14]

Christianity did little to dispel the belief in menstrual defilement: "Throughout its formative years, during the development of the great intellectual and doctrinal systems, Christianity clung to the Old Testament belief in the uncleanness of woman and the basically imperfect nature that was a consequence of the menstrual flow."[15]

The influence of religion on the practice of the intramenstrual taboo remains quite strong. Psychologist Karen Paige, after a study of sexual abstinence in menstruating Protestant, Catholic, and Jewish women in the United States, found that most Jews and Catholics reported *never* having sex during menstruation, while fewer than half the Protestant women reported similar behavior. Moreover, Paige notes, Orthodox Jewish women are prohibited from intercourse during menstruation and for seven days following, whereupon they must cleanse themselves through the ritual *mikvah*, or purifying bath. The Roman Catholic church, she continues, "also urges abstinence during a woman's period, and historically has promoted the view of woman as unclean vessel that tempts the pure man."[16] Indeed, in 1970, Levitical prohibitions were included in arguments justifying an American Roman Catholic decision against women serving in the sanctuary as lectors and commentators during the Mass.[17]

The modern American menstrual "aesthetic" which finds intercourse during menstruation "messy" or "undignified" (and therefore best forgone) is but the latest version of an ancestral theme.

> The United States does not relegate menstruating women to special huts, but we have our share of superstitions and the implicit belief lingers that the menstruating woman is unclean. Many couples abstain from sex during the woman's period. (A recent survey of 960 California families showed that half the men and women had *never* had sex during menstruation.)[18]

So pervasive is the sense of female "uncleanness" that women continue to internalize men's loathing. Coming to feel soiled, ugly, or contaminating, the menstruating woman is made conscious of her body *as a repulsive object to others*. Karen Paige notes:

> Women take great care to avoid any signs of menstruation, which would cause profound embarrassment to the woman and the observer—unlike a nosebleed or cut finger. Sanitary

22

napkin and tampon ads perpetuate, as they placate, such apprehensions, assuring the buyer she is safe from public humiliation. Women undergo considerable pressure to maintain high standards of "feminine hygiene" during the menstrual flow.[19]

The insidious effects of menstrual defilement on women themselves have been increasingly noted by feminists. Going beyond the work of mythologists, anthropologists, and psychiatrists who have duly recorded the presence of menstrual defilement, feminists have focused on the crippling psychological effects of patriarchy's characterization of the female body as polluting and dangerous. Adrienne Rich argues:

23

> . . . the menstrual cycle is yet another aspect of female experience which patriarchal thinking has turned inside out, rendering it sinister or disadvantageous. Internalizing this attitude, we actually perceive ourselves as polluted. Our tendency to flesh-loathing (the aversion to the female body passed on to us by men) is underscored; religious taboos are laid on us even in "advanced" societies. A man whose unconscious is saturated with the fear of menstrual blood will make a woman feel that her period is a time of pollution, the visitation of an evil spirit, physically repulsive.[20]

Apart from women's damaged self-image, the most serious effect of women's sense of uncleanness is the denial of specifically female power—body-centered and body-celebrated. Were women to understand menses as an element of the life force (the *mana* of blood, the *mana* of conception) they would regard themselves as wholly integrated, without contempt or shame for their body's mysteries. The time of menses would then give to the female body a respect and sense of wonder that women, following men, have denied it.

Whatever the concrete illustration of the menstrual taboo, women's blood signals a creative possibility lost to men. In the patriarchal mind, man, the one who does not bleed, is perceived as normal, ordinary, healthy; woman, the one who bleeds with frightening regularity, is necessarily alien, strange, diseased. Men's response has been dread and exclusion of women (the accursed), yet awe and reverence for women's life-giving power (the sacred).

The biological fact of menstruation has meant that women have not been trusted with serious social responsibility: economic, political, intellectual. Kept from elite councils and sacred rites, from political power and social authority, they have been denied primary value. On the relationship between menstrual pollution and women's subordinate position, Paige concludes:

> My current research on a sample of 114 societies around the world indicates that ritual observances and taboos about menstruation are a method of controlling women and their fertility. Men apparently use such rituals, along with those surrounding pregnancy and childbirth, to assert their claims to women and their children.[21]

As a clear example of the "naturalization" of women, menstrual defilement begins with woman's body, then fashions her social roles, and finally contaminates her psychology. The female body—smells, genitals, excretions—is unclean, polluting, dangerous. Consequently, woman is devalued and excluded from sociopolitical authority. The result is a damaged psyche: weak and self-denigrating, afflicted by the cycles of animal existence.[22]

Symbolic indicators such as menstrual defilement are sufficient to make the point of female inferiority in a given culture. Moreover, menstrual pollution is an excellent index since it connects the three kinds of evidence anthropologists find essential in determining women's cultural status: symbolic devaluation (mythology of the taboo), explicit devaluation (taboo itself), and sociostructural exclusion (isolation, secondary status, loss of authority). By interweaving all three, menstrual defilement reveals how domination becomes a *natural* aspect of individual and collective life through myth, religion, sociohistorical roles, and psychic formations.[23]

In displaying the range and subtlety of sexual politics, menstrual pollution serves as an incomparable example. But the true significance of menstrual defilement rests in the unconscious sources of its origins: fear, revulsion, and envy of the human body, later transmuted into patriarchal fear of the female body. Dorothy Dinnerstein argues that

> . . . human ambivalence toward the body of woman arises from, and at the same time helps perpetuate, incompetence to reconcile our inevitable mix of feelings for the flesh itself. The unreconciled mix is projected onto the first parent. Worse still, much of the positive side of this ambivalence is suppressed and what has been suppressed is converted into an obscene preoccupation; this means that even the love that is part of the prevailing attitude toward woman's body is to some degree a dirty love.[24]

24

Apart from a transformation of human sexuality, which is necessarily slow and experimental, a new and healthier sense of the body, of the *female body*, needs to be developed by women themselves. Part of this consciousness involves a purposeful representation of the menses as a unique, engendering force—a sensuous, transformative power, symbolic of life and life's continuity. With this celebration of the uniqueness of the female body, women would no longer feel shame or internalize their pollution. They would recover their bodies as the center rather than the prison of their beings: separate, different, powerful.

Ontology

Woman's experience of menstrual defilement is part of her ontology, an ontology which defines her as an intermediary between nature and culture, which shapes woman's experience of *being* by associating her with some "lower," physical world, the world of her body and its issue, children.

As I have argued, the organization of women's experience in the West follows a nature/culture dichotomy which legitimates women's restriction to the domestic sphere and the mothering role. Thus woman's experience of *being* is closely tied to her experiences as nurturer and lover.

But these experiences do not occur in isolation; they are lived within a patriarchal system which values man and his achievements over woman and her achievements. This valuation means that woman first comes to understand and know her Self through a hierarchical system in which she is subordinated to another, in which she is *not* the Self but the Other. Her consciousness and her potential are tainted by her subjugation *as the Other*. She suffers a colonized mentality.

The effect of patriarchal ideology, evidenced by the menstrual taboo, is precisely this colonized mentality, an experience of being-in-bondage. Perhaps more than the actual institutions that anchor women's oppression, the daily experience of this condition reveals the nature, the extent, and the subtlety of women's subjugation.

Brilliantly analyzed by Simone de Beauvoir, patriarchal ontology illustrates woman's intersubjective experience of being-in-bondage. Nature/Culture ideology is translated into an *experience* of subjugation: patriarchy on its most intimate, personal level. For women, this experience ranges from social inequality to sexual harassment and rape, from "institutionalized" motherhood to wife-beating and sexual slavery.

Under the patriarchal order, relations between the Self and the pluralities of the male world turn on degrees of domination. The life-struggle between the Self and the Other which continues the search for mutual recognition and which carries within itself the hope of reciprocity and equality is deformed in the relationship between men and women. Man defines the Self as his own being; he defines woman as Other, as Object. Simone de Beauvoir believes that

> . . . what peculiarly signalizes the situation of woman is that she—a free and autonomous being like all human creatures—nevertheless finds herself living in a world where men compel her to assume the status of the Other. They propose to stabilize her as object and to doom her to immanence since her transcendence is to be overshadowed and forever transcended by another ego (conscience) which is essential and sovereign. The drama of woman lies in this conflict between the fundamental aspirations of every subject (ego)— who always regards the Self as the essential—and the compulsions of a situation in which she is the inessential.[25]

Following de Beauvoir's ontology, we *are*, as individuals, only to the extent that we are recognized. Woman's identity, her consciousness of Self, is connected to her recognition by others, by men. She experiences her Self as "inessential" because she is recognized (in the Hegelian sense) *as* the "inessential" by man. (The lesbian-feminist concept of Woman-Identified-Woman can be seen as a recognition *by women* that they are primary and men are secondary. In this ontology, man is the "inessential," the Other.)

In his objectification of woman, man visualizes her in fear and desire, hoping to possess and use her as an extension of himself. Woman, being the "inessential" Other, identifies her Self as inessential. Before she can be independent and sovereign (unto herself, other women), she must first *see* herself as independent and sovereign; she must become conscious of her internalized "inauthentic" identity, which is nevertheless constantly reinforced by man's deformed recognition. Through patriarchal culture, he repudiates, negates her Self as independent. Thus woman's struggle against man's objectification and toward the creation of her own "authentic" identity becomes a continuous revelation of ever-deeper forms of Otherness.

26

Because the sexes are in unequal, exploitative relationship to each other, reciprocity (the process of mutual recognition) begins from an abnormal, sometimes pathological point. For example, the "ideal" form of interdependency in all love relationships (based on the memory of our first dependency within the mother-infant bond) is basically an expansion of reciprocity into protected, mutually experienced vulnerability. But this kind of interdependency assumes the possibility of mutual recognition, of a careful unfolding nurtured in trust and respect. When recognition is merely an acting out of gendered personalities and their attached sex-roles, the reciprocal process is stunted; interdependency takes on the taint of oppression. With the historical weight of patriarchal politics, relations between the sexes regress to a common pathology: the "feminine" woman is masochistic, the "masculine" man is sadistic.

Given this kind of sexual psychology, it is clear why woman's struggle into consciousness, into recognition as an independent self-consciousness, is often an embattled project, characterized by intense alienation, anguish, and bitterness. Like the colonized subject, woman suffers a collective identity which is predetermined, overdetermined. She is forever outside the dialectic—of consciousness, of recognition, of history.

Such predetermination is described by Hegel, Sartre, and Fanon.[26] Fanon's struggle, in particular, has much to contribute to an understanding of women's conditions. His fierce battle for identity was historically determined by colonization as women's struggle is determined by their historic subjugation to men.

> As he groped to understand who he was, when he confronted the image of himself which he discovered facing white Frenchmen, an image which in no sense corresponded to his own inner self-portrait, Fanon began to understand that he was either doomed to struggle, or to exist, not as he was, but as he appeared in the eyes of others. If the objective of struggle was clear . . . the process seemed to unravel unexpected layers of imposed otherness. The more he was to fight his way to the surface of this recognition, the more he realized that he fought as others locked in the bond of servitude peculiar to the historical relationship of blacks and whites, colonizer and colonized, oppressors and oppressed.[27]

Fanon perceived the project of consciousness for blacks as a double, interlocking process: one had to struggle against the master (the white world), *and* against one's Self who would be like the master. In distinguishing these conflicts, Fanon accounted for the alleged "dependency" complex of the colonized. He also exposed the continuing racism of white psychologists who justified colonization on the doubtful grounds that mutual psychological needs were satisfied: the need of the European to be master, the need of the African to be servant.[28]

Fanon's insights—that oppression creates a servile pathology in the oppressed and a legitimating psychology in the oppressor—now form part of the standard analysis of oppressive relationships. In the case of women, the analogies are obvious. The more woman struggles against patriarchy, its institutions and ideology, the more she finds her struggle to be an internal one. The ideological chain in women's hearts and minds—the repression of their anger, the masochism of their self-images, the helpless pregnability that is their physical sense—circles back, farther and farther, to the earliest days of infancy. The psychology of the family (asymmetrical parenting: female childcare) fashions an identity (asymmetrical gender: "dominant" masculine, "subordinate" feminine) which is supported by the sexual division of labor into domestic and public realms. Domination by the public, "masculine" world is elaborated and reproduced through the social superego: the educational-legal system, the complex of religious and philosophical views, the organization of scientific and bureaucratic work. In the end, patriarchy prevails because its mechanisms of reproduction are implanted within its victims: male and female alike. For both, the patriarchal process is akin to the colonizing process. Kate Millett was one of the first American feminists to point to the "colonization" of women.

> What goes largely unexamined, often even unacknowledged (yet is institutionalized nonetheless) in our social order, is the birthright priority whereby males rule females. Through this system a most ingenious form of "interior colonization" has been achieved. It is one which tends moreover to be sturdier than any form of segregation, and more rigorous than class stratification, more uniform, certainly more enduring. However muted its present appearance may be, sexual dominion obtains nevertheless as perhaps the most pervasive ideology of our culture and provides its most fundamental concept of power.[29]

For women coming to consciousness, especially radical self-consciousness, the comparison of women and colonized peoples is a first attempt at perspective—historic, social, personal. In 1974, Robin Morgan, a New York feminist, tried to articulate women's oppression beyond the issues of class, race, and caste. She alighted, temporarily, on colonization.

> Women are a colonized people. Our history, values, and *cross-cultural culture* have been taken from us—a gynocidal attempt manifest most arrestingly in the patriarchal seizure of our basic and precious "land": our bodies.
>
> Our bodies have been taken from us, mined for their natural resources (sex and children), and deliberately mystified. Five thousand years of Judeo-Christian tradition, virulent in its misogyny, have helped enforce the attitude that women are "unclean." Androcentric medical science, like other professional industries in the service of the patriarchal colonizer, has researched better and more efficient means of *mining* our natural resources, with (literally) bloody little concern for the true health, comfort, nurturance, or even survival of those resources. This should hardly surprise us; our ignorance about our own primary terrain—our bodies—is in the self-interest of the patriarchy.[30]

29

The sense of loss, followed by anger, then rage, at the discovery of "interior colonization" is exactly the process of coming to consciousness through others' oppressive identification. In de Beauvoir's terms, before woman can make her projects in and through the world, she must encounter her own flesh-loathing, her own masochistic self-sacrifice, her own willing subjugation to "institutionalized motherhood." If this confrontation is successful, though never complete, the subsequent response is anger, then rage. In her project of consciousness, Morgan reflects an historic development out of sexual oppression: the feminist revolution.

Through the feminist methodology of consciousness-raising, feminists have investigated their own experience of being, but being as a woman, not being as an abstract male entity. This exploration has revealed, as de Beauvoir predicted, that "woman" is a social construction. Examinations of women's gender roles, especially mothering, and women's status under law, custom, and kinship uncover again and again that woman's situation is connected to her definition as a sex. In Catharine MacKinnon's words, "feminist inquiry into women's own experience of sexuality revises prior comprehensions of sexual issues and transforms the concept of sexuality itself—its determinants and its role in society and politics." This revision, MacKinnon continues, has brought the understanding that one becomes a woman "through the experience of sexuality: a complex unity of physicality, emotionality, identity, and status affirmation." This experience is as sexual object/victim of men.[31]

If patriarchy, broadly defined, is a system of male power over women, and if women's place in this system is as sexual object, then the experience of this system *from women's perspective* is one of "male pursuit of control over women's sexuality." The feminist issues here are familiar: prostitution, pornography, rape, abortion, incest, contraception, sexual harassment. All these are "women's issues" because they all connect to sexuality. Feminist praxis has led to a feminist political theory: sexuality and its "social determination, daily construction, birth to death expression, and ultimate male control."[32]

MacKinnon's analysis of the centrality of sexuality in women's oppression focuses the ontological experiences of women. Like the colonized subject, woman exists in a world where power is defined and refined as domination. In de Beauvoir's terms, she is "inauthentic" and "inessential" because she is controlled and objectified by man. For women, the power of self-definition, of "authenticity," is limited if not crushed.

Under male supremacy, then, power *is* domination (just as woman's experience of sexuality *is* her experience of powerlessness). In Adrienne Rich's terms: "Power is both a primal word and a primal relationship under patriarchy. . . . [F]rom very ancient times the identity . . . of the man depends on power, and on power in a certain, specific sense: that of *power over others*."[33] The concept of "power over" captures the impelling force of patriarchy: an appropriation of people and things in man's search for meaning and expression. Rich elaborates:

> . . . women have experienced "power over" in two forms, both of them negative. The first is men's power over us—whether physical, economic, or institutional—along with the spectacle of their bloody struggles for power over other men, their implicit sacrifice of human relationships and emotional values in the quest for dominance.[34]

As the core value of patriarchy, "power over" begins with the power of men to control women's sexuality and to fashion social institutions from that control. The tyrannies of father over son, and elder male over younger, are built from the initial victory of male over female. Once the patriarchal design—dominance/subordinance—is played out between the sexes, it is endlessly reenacted in the murderous conflicts—psychic, social, historical—between men, among brothers, within the fraternity. Witness the patriarchal vision.

Freud's mythic horde revolves around an archetypal struggle with the castrating father later killed by his jealous sons, who then possess his property in common, including all women. Locke's contractarian brotherhood arises in opposition to the despotism of the natural father and his patriarchal family: "egalitarian" society is egalitarian because man's properties (his person, the fruits of his labor, his women and children) are protected from other men. Aristotle's polity is built from the patriarchal household: the rule of man over woman, parent over child, master over slave. His model of government is familial domination.[35] No matter how solidarity between men is established—through Freudian guilt, Lockean contract, Aristotelian citizenship—civilization is seen to develop from male groupings. Women, the first victims, are not members of the patriarchal fraternity; they are its property, the sexual spoils of war.

Notes

1. For a poetic elaboration of the relationship between women and nature, see Susan Griffin, *Woman and Nature: The Roaring Inside Her* (New York: Harper and Row, 1978). See also Carolyn Merchant, *The Death of Nature: Woman, Ecology and the Scientific Revolution* (New York: Harper and Row, 1980).

2. Sherry Ortner, "Is Female to Male as Nature Is to Culture?" in *Woman, Culture and Society*, ed. Michelle Rosaldo and Louise Lamphere (Stanford: Stanford University Press, 1974), p. 71.

3. See Peggy Sanday, *Female Power and Male Dominance* (New York: Cambridge University Press, 1981); and Merchant, *The Death of Nature*.

4. Ortner, "Is Female to Male as Nature Is to Culture?" p. 73.

5. See Michelle Rosaldo, "Woman, Culture and Society: A Theoretical Overview," in *Woman, Culture and Society*, pp. 17–42.

6. Ortner, "Is Female to Male as Nature Is to Culture?" p. 81.

7. Nancy Chodorow, *The Reproduction of Mothering* (Berkeley: University of California Press, 1978).

8. See Joseph Campbell, *The Masks of God*, 4 vols. (New York: Viking, 1964); H. R. Hays, *The Dangerous Sex: The Myth of Feminine Evil* (New York: Putnam, 1964); Jane Harrison, *Mythology* (New York: Harcourt Brace, 1963); C. J. Jung, *Man and His Symbols* (London: Aldus, 1964) and *The Archetypes and the Collective Unconscious* (New York: Pantheon, 1959).

9. For an excellent account of the place of women in Christian theology, see Rosemary Radford Reuther's "Misogynism and Virginal Feminism in the Fathers of the Church," in *Religion and Sexism: Images of Woman in the Jewish and Christian Traditions* (New York: Simon and Schuster, 1974), pp. 150–183. See also, in the same volume, Phyllis Bird, "Images of Women in the Old Testament," pp. 41–89; Judith Hauptman, "Images of Women in the Talmud," pp. 184–212; Bernard Prusak, "Woman: Seductive Siren and Source of Sin," pp. 98–116.

10. Joseph Campbell, *The Masks of God: Primitive Mythology* (New York: Viking, 1972), pp. 59–60.

11. For an excellent history of the menstrual taboo, see Janice Delaney, Mary Jane Lupton, and Emily Toth, *The Curse: A Cultural History of Menstruation* (New York: Mentor Books, 1976), p. 1.

12. Ibid. See also Mary Douglas, *Purity and Danger* (New York: Harper, 1966); William Stephens, *A Cross-Cultural Study of Menstrual Taboos* (Provincetown, Mass.: Psychological Monographs, 1961); Bruno Bettelheim, *Symbolic Wounds: Puberty Rites and the Envious Male* (New York: Collier, 1962); Ian Hogbin, *The Island of Menstruating Men* (San Francisco: Chandler, 1970); Hutton Webster, *Taboo: A Sociological Study* (Stanford: Stanford University Press, 1942); James George Frazer, *The Golden Bough*, vol. 1 (New York: Macmillan, 1953); Paula Weideger, *Menstruation and Menopause* (New York: Dell, 1977).

13. See Adrienne Rich's discussion of this fact from personal communications with women in Israel, in *Of Woman Born* (New York: Norton, 1976), p. 106.

14. For the entire citation, see Leviticus 15:19–33.

15. Delaney, Lupton, and Toth, *The Curse*, p. 35.

16. Karen Paige, "Women Learn to Sing the Menstrual Blues," in *Psychology Today*, September 1973, pp. 43–45.

17. Cited in Delaney, Lupton, and Toth, *The Curse*, p. 34.

18. Paige, "Women Learn to Sing the Menstrual Blues," p. 44.

19. Ibid., p. 45.

20. Rich, *Of Woman Born*, p. 106.

21. Paige, "Women Learn to Sing the Menstrual Blues," p. 47.

22. See Weideger, *Menstruation and Menopause*.

23. See Ortner, "Is Female to Male as Nature Is to Culture?"

24. Dorothy Dinnerstein, *The Mermaid and the Minotaur* (New York: Harper, 1976), p. 148.

25. Simone de Beauvoir, *The Second Sex* (New York: Knopf, 1953), p. xxviii.

26. See Georg Hegel, *The Phenomenology of Mind*, trans. J. B. Baillie (New York: Harper, 1967); Jean-Paul Sartre, *Being and Nothingness*, trans. H. Barnes (New York: Citadel Press, 1969), and *Anti-Semite and Jew*, trans. G. J. Becker (New York: Schocken Books, 1965); Frantz Fanon, *Black Skin, White Masks*, trans. Charles Markmann (New York: Grove Press, 1967), *The Wretched of the Earth*, trans. C. Farrington (New York: Grove Press, 1966), and *Toward the African Revolution*, trans. H. Chevalier (New York: Grove Press, 1968). For a good criticism of de Beauvoir and her reliance on patriarchal "Hegelian ontology," see Nancy Hartsock, *Money, Sex and Power* (New York: Longman, 1983), pp. 286–292.

27. Irene L. Gendzier, *Frantz Fanon* (New York: Vintage Books, 1973), p. 24. This is an excellent study of the man and his times, with an especially lucid analysis of Fanon's use of Hegel's and Sartre's discussion of the Master/Servant, Self/Other ontology.

28. Both Fanon's *Black Skin* and *Wretched* answer the racist defenses of colonialism epitomized in Fanon's time by O. Mannoni's *Prospero and Caliban*, trans. P. Powesland (New York: Praeger, 1964).

29. Kate Millet, *Sexual Politics* (New York: Avon, 1971), p. 25.

30. Robin Morgan, *Going Too Far: The Personal Chronicle of a Feminist* (New York: Random House, 1977), p. 161.

31. Catharine MacKinnon, "Feminism, Marxism, Method and the State," in *Feminist Theory: A Critique of Ideology*, ed. Nannerl Keohane, Michelle Rosaldo, Barbara Gelpi (Chicago: University of Chicago Press, 1982), p. 17.

32. Ibid.

33. Rich, *Of Woman Born*, p. 64.

34. Ibid., p. 68.

35. My analysis draws on Norman O. Brown, *Love's Body* (New York: Vintage Books, 1966). However, Brown defends this reality of patriarchy as brutal domination, where I use his insights for opposite purposes, as will be clear.

Two · Sociology

The necessary, peaceful link between fraternities is brought about through the systematic exchange of one form of property, women. Thus does exogamy enable society, construct its basic order, kinship. The incest taboo, with other social proscriptions, reinforces the exchange. Norman O. Brown, in his defense of patriarchy, has written:

> [There is] a connection between fraternal organization and exogamy, conceived as form of "marriage by capture." The band of brothers feel the incest taboo and the lure of strange women; and adopt military organization (gang organization) for purposes of rape. *Politics as gang bang.* The game is juvenile, or, as Freud would say, infantile; and deadly serious; it is the game of Eros and Thanatos; of sex and war.[1] (Italics Added)

The "sexual understructure" is nothing but the forced exchange of women "mined for their natural resources (sex and children)." Fraternal organization leads to military organization *for the purposes of rape.* Patriarchy ("politics") as brutal domination ("gang bang"); sexuality as violation, love as domination; sexual politics. Eros (love-life, symbolized by sex) is perverted by Thanatos (aggression-death, symbolized by war). The battleground of patriarchy *is* the body of woman.

In her monumental history of rape, Susan Brownmiller recounts the "deadly serious" game of patriarchy, locating the *original* act of subjugation in man's violation of woman's body. Behind the social contract, the tribe, the brotherhood, is rape, the first and most basic expression of "power over."

> It seems eminently sensible to hypothesize that man's violent capture and rape of the female led first to the establishment of a rudimentary mate-protectorate and then sometime later to the full-blown male solidification of power, the patriarchy. As the first permanent acquisition of man, his first piece of real property, woman was, in fact, the original building block, the cornerstone, of the "house of the father." Man's

forcible extension of his boundaries to his mate and later to their offspring was the beginning of his concept of ownership. Concepts of hierarchy, slavery, and private property flowed from and could only be predicated upon the initial subjugation of woman.[2]

36

Both Brown and Brownmiller have taken the pulse of patriarchy: fraternal organization and the achievement of manhood are defined by, and depend upon, misogyny; upon the extent and success of man's domination of woman as wife, as supporter, as servant, but primarily as sexual object/victim. Thus the reality of man's hatred and fear of women is told through the record of patriarchal crime—sexual slavery, incest, clitoridectomy, infibulation, footbinding, prostitution, witch hunts, child molestation, even rape within marriage. The sexual understructure is protected by patriarchal violence.[3]

The link between exogamy and rape is clear. Given its origins and purposes, exogamy means much more than kinship. For women, exogamy is a regulated form of transfer of their bodies and its products. Beyond the mate-protectorate, exogamy simply means that a certain man has exclusive rights to the body of a certain woman. The fundamental, social significance of these rights accounts for the definition of rape (customary and legal) as a crime of property rather than a crime of violence. Historically, rape has never been viewed as a violation of the person. It has always been seen as a violation of one man's property (woman) by another man. This, and not money or land, explains why marriage is a property relationship. Institutionally, marriage has protected a man's right to his wife's body. Historically, marriage is but one socially acceptable form of rape.[4]

In anthropological terms, the impact of the exchange of women, their objectification as gifts, is clear: men control women, sexual dominion is anchored in social structure. Lévi-Strauss has argued: "The reciprocal bond basic to marriage is not set up between men and women, but between men and men by means of women, who are only the principle occasion for it."[5] The relationship between women and men is that between gift and giver, object and owner. Regardless of women's valuation (and women are enormously valued because they reproduce the species), they remain the *objects* of exchange. In terms of power, the relationship between men and women is forever unequal, freighted with oppression; it is the ancient bondage between ruler and ruled. Anthropologist Gayle Rubin notes:

The result of a gift of women is more profound than the result of other gift transactions, because the relationship thus established is not just one of reciprocity but one of kinship. . . . Kinship is organization, and organization gives power. . . . As long as the relations specify that men exchange women, it is men who are the beneficiaries of the product of such exchanges—social organizations.[6]

37

Both Lévi-Strauss and Rubin have been criticized by Marxist theorist Nancy Hartsock. She has called Lévi-Strauss's argument on the exchange of women a "phallocratic mystification of women's material lives" which locates "women's oppression in the sphere of ideology rather than material social relations."[7] Moreover, Rubin's use of Lévi-Strauss is described as "abstract determinism" by Hartsock, who persuasively argues that both anthropologists stress cultural categories (e.g., women as "signs" who are made "taboo") over the experience of daily life as the source of women's oppression.[8]

Hartsock's critical approach is made from a Marxist feminist perspective. In pointing to the need for specificity and concreteness, she focuses the question of why women are exchanged. She asks, in rebuttal to Lévi-Strauss and Rubin: Why are women exchange commodities to begin with? And she answers: Surely not because they are "signs." Rather, she argues, it is the sexual division of labor where women care for children that has determined their exchange status.

To my mind, Hartsock's analysis leads back from the heights of Lévi-Strauss's myth-and-sign-making to the daily construction of women's reproductive capacities. Women are indeed exchanged, but not because of their mysterious signification. They are exchanged because they reproduce the species, because they continue and thereby ensure life. In this view, biology is transformed by concrete relationships (the sexual division of labor) into a daily experience of subordination.

And so it is that women are the lifeblood of a people, their magical symbols of immortality. Women are defined and confined by their power to bring forth. Before the discovery of paternity, woman was the only certain source of life. Once paternity was known, she became the most prized possession of men. On women's place in agrarian societies, sociologist Meda Chesney-Lind has written:

They are used to form alliances between different patriarchal units and produce progeny for these particular kinship groups.

Thus, in settled agrarian society, women's childbearing capacity dictates their status. . . . Women became, in a sense, sexual property within an almost universal patriarchal system.[9]

This function does not alter in industrial societies, despite the family's changed structure (from extended to nuclear) and diminished productivity (from a center of production to a center of consumption). Thus, in linking groups and ensuring heirs, women are enslaved to the species.

And this enslavement is culturally instituted. Despite the obvious burdens of maternity, woman's bondage to man is only facilitated, not foreordained, by her biology. Painfully, woman's historic condition reflects a pool of oppression. Subordination is blatant (as in institutional oppression—exclusive female child-care), yet insidious (as in psychological oppression—overdependence). From infancy, socialization processes point to motherhood as the supreme aim of woman's life. Religion, popular mythology, and the language of patriotism nourish an "inevitable" choice. Finally, through a confluence of forces—legal, economic, and educational discrimination; sociopolitical exclusion; ideological justification—motherhood becomes an institutional reality. "Biological" mothering *engenders* "emotional" mothering: an anguished because unrelieved source of love and self-sacrifice for the child, the man, the nation. Adrienne Rich has pointed out:

> Institutionalized motherhood demands of women maternal "instinct" rather than intelligence, selflessness rather than self-realization, relation to others rather than the creation of self. . . . Patriarchy would seem to require, not only that women shall assume the major burden of pain and self-denial for the furtherance of the species, but that a majority of that species—women—shall remain essentially unquestioning and unenlightened. On this "underemployment" of female consciousness depend the morality and the emotional life of the human family.[10]

Significantly, the amazing strength and awareness of emotional mothering is consistently blunted by a patriarchal culture which fears and reveres the Great Earth Mother.[11] The deplorable effect is that strong women are rendered psychologically and economically dependent. In patriarchal culture, strength is destructive, dependence crippling. But in the mother's relationship with the child, strength is generative, dependence supportive. There is an essential conflict between the mother-child unit, and the larger patriarchal family of which it is part. Under a system of sexual dominion, repudiation of our "mother" values is necessary for the embrace of our "father" values. In the metaphor of classic psychoanalysis, "Oedipal" development must replace "pre-Oedipal" development. Mythologically, patriarchy needs to subordinate matriarchy.

But the mother prevails. Our preconscious attachment to her and all that is warm, secure, and eternal creates the desire of our emotional needs and fashions the gaze of our loving eye. Knowingly, psychoanalysis, with mythology, condemns the patriarchal triumph: Oedipus fails to recognize his mother, the repressed returns in a tragic denouement.

The connection between parental conflict, the legacy of each new generation of mothers and fathers, and the persistence of exogamy is clear. As long as women are exchanged, the "kingdom of the fathers"—the public realm—passes to the sons. The "sacred calling of the mothers"—the domestic realm—is bequeathed to the daughters. The sexual division of labor, writ large, is precisely this division between the "kingdom of the fathers" and the "sacred calling of the mothers." In sociological terms, exogamy reveals that women are not *true* inheritors; they serve only as the bloodline *between* inheritors.

For many anthropologists, exogamy is the cornerstone of Western civilization, the basic organizational form from which all other cultural forms radiate. If this is accurate, then exogamy enables Western civilization. Rephrased: without the objectification, sexual constraint, and systematic exchange of women, Western civilization would be impossible. Freud's theory recapitulated in Lévi-Strauss's anthropology: the oppression of women is necessary for Western civilization.

But the question remains: What kind of civilization? If it is true that women are *always* subordinated to men, that social authority always belongs to men, then Western civilization, *as we know it*, has been patriarchal. Therefore, the wellsprings of patriarchy must be the grounding of this civilization. Sexual dominion, the power of men over women, is not merely an agent of culture, it is the origin and conduit of culture.

The perspective of the id (psychoanalysis) confirms that of the superego (anthropology): the repressive organization of human sexuality enables Western civilization. In returning to Freud's analysis, we recall that instinctual repression is the basis of Western civilization. Given this assumption, the organization of repression underlies *all* Western societies. The form of each level (the given sociohistorical organization of reality) varies from age to age. What does not vary is the *fact* of repressive organization.

> It has been argued that Freud's . . . analysis of the repressive transformation of the instincts under the impact of the reality principle generalizes from a specific historical form of reality to reality pure and simple. This criticism is valid, but its validity does not vitiate the truth in Freud's generalization, namely, that a repressive organization of the instincts underlies *all* historical forms of the reality principle in civilization. . . . He expresses the historical fact that civilization has progressed as organized *domination*. This awareness guides his entire phylogenetic construction, which derives civilization from the replacement of the patriarchal despotism of the primal horde by the internalized despotism of the brother clan. Precisely because all civilization has been organized domination, the historical development assumes the dignity and necessity of a universal biological development.[12]

Marcuse's insight here is especially, although inadvertently, meaningful for the oppression of women. While underscoring the conjunction between biology and history as the result of the dominating nature of civilization, Marcuse has revealed the character of that domination as *male*: first paternal, then fraternal. Although Marcuse later argues for a matriarchal stage between the primal horde and the brother clan, the reality of male domination points to the original foundation of the repressive organization of sexuality: women as individuals, and as symbols of human and physical nature. With the progression of history, the specifics of this organization become cultural imperatives "assuming the dignity and necessity of a universal biological development." Thus the "sexual understructure" of patriarchy is nothing less than the (assumed "biological") forms of human life: the exchange of women, the sexual division of labor, exclusive gender division, obligatory heterosexuality.

While women's secondary status is everywhere confirmed, the subtle chain which binds their hearts and minds is often lost against the magnitude of history. Beginning with apparent fundamentals of human nature, the "sexual understructure" links physiology with sociology, and sociology with psychology. We are transformed by a psychology based in the body: body interpenetrates mind, which creates society. Linkages are subtle, connections harmonious. Indeed, sexual institutions appear so uniform, they are often understood as products of nature rather than culture.

While no single cultural form can be said to supersede all others in significance, the sexual division of labor approaches central importance. For here, where tasks and achievements divide between the sexes, differences come to have unequal consequences, and thereby exaggerated expression.

41

Because of tremendous cultural diversity in the actual tasks assigned by sex, anthropologists generally agree that it is the *fact* of the sexual division of labor, rather than its specific form, which is required by human groups. According to Lévi-Strauss, "the sexual division of labor is nothing else than a device to institute a reciprocal state of dependency between the sexes."[13]

Considering men's primary cultural status and the psychological effects of inequality, Lévi-Strauss's claim of reciprocity is doubtful.[14] Men and women may need each other, and this need may be elaborated and justified through the division of labor, but the uneven social valuation which attaches to labor arrangements renders any judgment of reciprocity false. Moreover, the anthropological definition of reciprocity (an exchange of equally valued objects) does not apply between men and women. Reciprocity applies only between men, because they are the exchangers of women. Given the asymmetrical nature of gender systems as well as the cultural superiority of men, a reciprocal state of dependency between the sexes is all but impossible, for this kind of reciprocity implies a mutual recognition and respect, the hope, if not the immediate possibility, of an equality of status. "Reciprocal dependency" is really "interdependency"—an interlocking of lives founded in continual trust and care, in mutual nurturance. Between men and women, however, there is little or no equality. The resulting power imbalance precludes true reciprocity in all but the most creative and "care-full" of relationships. Thus is the division of labor, like wisdom and love, everywhere unequally valued for men and for women. Margaret Mead argues: "One aspect of the social valuation of different types of labor is the differential prestige of men's activities and women's activities. Whatever men do— even if it is dressing dolls for religious ceremonies—is more prestigious than what women do and is treated as a higher achievement."[15]

But if the state of dependency is hardly reciprocal between the sexes, the resulting socioeconomic unit of one woman and one man does serve a particular organizing purpose. The sexual division of labor splits the sexes into exclusive categories (GENDER) while forbidding same-sex unions (HOMOSEXU-ALITY). The argument has been constructed by Gayle Rubin. In tracing the logic of the organization of sexuality, Rubin notes that homosexuality is not simply prohibited, nor is heterosexuality simply encouraged. Specific cultural forms appear in considerable variety, such as cross-cousin marriage, mandatory (but temporary) homosexual unions, bridewealth (which enables both men and women to take same-sex spouses), and gender transformations replete with cross-sex privileges. Despite variations, however, the norm is everywhere protected: exclusive gender divisions and heterosexual unions. The protection of those norms suggests that they are far from naturally occurring products of our biology. Needing the cultural reinforcement of the sexual division of labor, they appear to be carefully ensured social prescriptions. "If biological and hormonal imperatives were as overwhelming as popular mythology would have them, it would hardly be necessary to insure heterosexual union by means of economic interdependency."[16]

Rubin's insight points to the related nature of patriarchal imperatives. The sexual division of labor (particularly female child-care) exacerbates biological differences between the sexes, thus creating gender. In turn, gender identifies the sexes as separate yet complementary. Not only is heterosexuality ensured, but homosexuality is proscribed.

> Gender is not only an identification with one sex; it also entails that sexual desire be directed toward the other sex. The sexual division of labor is implicated in both aspects of gender—male and female it creates them, and it creates them heterosexual. The suppression of the homosexual component of human sexuality, and by corollary, the oppression of homosexuals, is therefore a product of the same system whose rules and relations oppress women.[17]

Psychologically, the command of exclusive gender identity necessitates the repression of natural similarities and an exaggeration of natural differences. In terms of personality development and expression, this means a denial of "feminine" behavior in men and "masculine" behavior in women, however these categories are culturally defined.

> The division of the sexes has the effect of repressing some of the personality characteristics of virtually everyone, men and women. The same social system which oppresses women

42

in its relations of exchange, oppresses everyone in its insistence upon a rigid division of personality.[18]

The *social* rule of gender division creates the *psychological* rule of personality division. Patriarchal social organization is supported by repressive psychologies in both women and men. Polarized and unequal personalities (gender) facilitate internal control, safeguarding the patriarchal order more effectively than any external force.

In her tortuous rehabilitation of Freud, Juliet Mitchell worked out the unnerving connections between patriarchy and psychic formations:

> Freud's analysis of the psychology of women takes place within . . . an analysis of patriarchy. . . . Freud shows quite explicitly that the psychoanalytic concept of the unconscious is a concept of mankind's transmission and inheritance of his social (cultural) laws. . . . Understanding the laws of the unconscious thus amounts to a start in understanding how ideology functions, how we acquire and live the ideas and laws within which we must exist. A primary aspect of the law is that we live according to our sexed identity, our ever imperfect "masculinity" or "femininity."[19]

In accepting Freud's "primal horde" theory, Mitchell acknowledges the Oedipus complex as "certainly a patriarchal myth" because it reiterates the rule of the totem (no one may kill [eat] the symbolic father) and of exogamy (everyone must exchange the primal father's inheritance—women). Within this myth of the unconscious, the boy learns that he is heir to the father's law (patriarchy), while the girl learns her place within the law (subordination).

Despite Mitchell's rejection of major feminist reactions to Freud, her logic distills from his analysis conclusions very like those of de Beauvoir, Millett, and others. In simplified terms, Mitchell argues that since both sexes are born into patriarchal culture, both sexes desire to be like the father, that is, to assume his primary place and his active (transcendent) character. Of course, the way in which each child comes to experience this desire (symbolic castration for the boy, symbolic seduction for the girl) can and has been disputed, and so too the primary importance of the phallus and of each child's desire to possess the mother.

But given her orthodox Freudianism, Mitchell nevertheless returns to the cultural reality of male dominance. Her explana-

43

tion of "femininity" as a distorted personality form depends on her recognition that only the boy is allowed to assume the father's place. The girl enters the "man's world" at the will and in the specific fashion dictated by her father (i.e., by culture). As Mitchell observes, the implications of "femininity" are repudiated by both sexes. Both the boy and the girl learn that "femininity" entails *powerlessness* (a giving up of action and liberty); and that "masculinity" promises *power* (the pursuit of action and liberty). De Beauvoir would say that the "feminine" is understood as the immanent Other, the "masculine" as the transcendent Self. Thus does gender set the trajectory for women's oppression. Mitchell shares at least this one insight with contemporary feminists: the value of Freud's work is to be found in his charting of the corrosive effects of domination on the development of the female personality.

In expanding the insights of Lévi-Strauss and Freud, Rubin and Mitchell have suggested that the domination of men, and the socioeconomic and psychic oppression of women are directly traced to the organization of human sexuality. Biology is transformed by the sexual division of labor, currently expressed through the modern nuclear family. Psychically, the enculturation of the human infant involves a complicated unconscious journey (pre-Oedipal and Oedipal stages) which occurs under patriarchal conditions (asymmetrical parenting). These conditions and the consequent resolution of psychic processes are inherently oppressive to women, even while women's mediating function in civilization is valued.

Structurally, exogamy guarantees the objectification and exchange of women and the sociopolitical authority of men. Meanwhile, the sexual division of labor (particularly institutionalized motherhood) reproduces exclusive and asymmetrical gender, thereby ensuring heterosexuality. "Masculine" and "feminine" identities are imprinted on our unconscious through the incest taboo, giving psychic force to cultural norms. Finally, women's sexuality is constrained lest the entire system collapse from a repudiation of men's power. Gayle Rubin has argued:

> From the standpoint of the system, the preferred female sexuality would be one which responded to the desire of others, rather than one which actively desired and sought a response. . . . What would happen if our hypothetical woman not only refused the man to whom she was promised, but asked for a woman instead? If a single refusal were disruptive, a double refusal would be insurrectionary. If each woman is

44

promised to some man, neither has a right to dispose of herself. If two women managed to extricate themselves from the debt nexus, two other women would have to be found to take their place. As long as men have rights in women that they do not have in themselves, it would be sensible to expect that homosexuality in women would be subject to more suppression than in men.[20]

In the West, the roots of male control which Rubin describes attain their first growth within the triangle of the nuclear family. Apart from reproducing and socializing children, the family is the main form through which women participate in collective life. Here, the sexual division of labor appears as a justification for the restriction of women to certain tasks, reified as "domestic" contributions. Here too, women's erotic/reproductive characterization encourages their primary responsibility for the "emotional" life of family members. And as the public world becomes ever more impersonal and brutal (as Thanatos triumphs in the abuse of the environment, the slaughter of the weak, and the proliferation of destructive technology), the family beckons as a haven—tense, contradictory, and traumatic, but a haven nevertheless.

Consisting of two parents and their children, the family as we know it today is but the latest form of the sexual understructure. That is, social structure has evolved from extended kinship systems into relatively isolated nuclear units: the modern family.

This historical change underlies the commonplace and scholarly observation that women's lives are defined by the family. The anthropological argument that women's sphere is primarily the domestic realm while men's sphere is primarily the public realm supports our larger social sense that women are attached to the family and invest more of their time and take more of their emotional and creative satisfaction from the family than men do. This is partly explained by women's historical responsibility for child-care, which occurs within the family (while the child-tending responsibility itself is explained by the sexual division of labor). But women's restriction to the family is also explained by their systematic and near total exclusion from authority and achievement in the public realm.

Nevertheless, the obvious perception of women's symbiotic association with the family tends to obscure the exact institutions responsible for women's oppressed, subordinate condition. The family is not the final cause of women's subjugation.

Rather, the family is but the form, the shell which surrounds and enables the "sexual understructure."

Notes

1. Norman O. Brown, *Love's Body* (New York: Vintage Books, 1966), p. 15.

2. Susan Brownmiller, *Against Our Will: Men, Women and Rape* (New York: Bantam, 1976), pp. 7–8.

3. For an analysis of patriarchal crime, apart from Brownmiller's account, see Mary Daly, *Gyn/Ecology: The Metaethics of Radical Feminism* (Boston: Beacon, 1978), especially "The Sado-Ritual Syndrome: The Re-enactment of Goddess Murder," which covers Indian *suttee*, Chinese footbinding, African genital mutilation, European witch-burnings, American gynecology, and Nazi medicine (pp. 107–312).

4. Brownmiller, *Against Our Will*, pp. 6–22.

5. Claude Lévi-Strauss, *Elementary Structures of Kinship* (Boston: Beacon, 1969), p. 116.

6. Gayle Rubin, "The Traffic in Women," in *Toward an Anthropology of Women*, ed. Rayna Reiter (New York: Monthly Review Press, 1975), p. 173.

7. Nancy Hartsock, *Money, Sex and Power: Toward a Feminist Historical Materialism* (New York: Longman, 1983), pp. 267–268.

8. Ibid., p. 293.

9. Meda Chesney-Lind, "Motherhood as Option or Destiny?" (Diss., University of Hawaii, 1977), p. 9.

10. Adrienne Rich, *Of Woman Born* (New York: Norton, 1976), pp. 42–43.

11. See Erich Neumann, *The Great Mother* (Princeton: Princeton University Press, 1972).

12. Herbert Marcuse, *Eros and Civilization* (Boston: Beacon, 1966), p. 34.

13. Lévi-Strauss, *Elementary Structures of Kinship*, pp. 347–348.

14. See Ronald V. Samson's study of the psychological effects of inequality in relationships and the transformation of a "reciprocal state of dependency" into psychological bondage, in *The Psychology of Power* (New York: Random House, 1969).

15. Margaret Mead, "Prehistory and the Woman," *Barnard College Bulletin*, April 30, 1969, Supplement, p. 7.

16. Rubin, "The Traffic in Women," p. 10.

17. Ibid., p. 180.

18. Ibid.

19. Juliet Mitchell, *Psycho-analysis and Feminism* (New York: Vintage Books, 1974), pp. 402–403.

20. Rubin, "The Traffic in Women," pp. 182–183. See also Adrienne Rich, "Compulsory Heterosexuality and Lesbian Existence," in *Signs* 5, no. 4 (Summer 1980); and a critique of Rich's argument in Ann Ferguson, Jacquelyn N. Zita, and Kathryn Pyne Addelson, "On 'Compulsory Heterosexuality and Lesbian Existence': Defining the Issues," in *Feminist Theory: A Critique of Ideology*, ed. Nannerl Keohane, Michelle Rosaldo, and Barbara Gelpi (Chicago: University of Chicago Press, 1982), pp. 147–188.

47

Three · History

Capitalism, the Modern Family, and the Separation of Life from Work

Until the Middle Ages, social organization was based on kinship, which organized sex and gender, thereby organizing society. Before the appearance of the nuclear family, kinship systems were responsible for basic needs, the regulation of sexuality, the distribution of power, and the determination of social relationships. In a phrase, kinship constituted society. The modern separation of the conjugal unit from other units did not exist. Indeed, clan communities or age-groups were often more central to a society than a unit of parents and children. As a separate entity, the conjugal unit is of recent vintage. In anthropological terms, this has meant a reduction of the kinship structure to the nuclear family. Kinship functions have been taken over by the "economy" (large-scale material production), by schools, and by bureaucratic organizations. The sexual understructure, once integrated into the fabric of life through the encompassing kinship system, collapsed into the family because the significance of kinship itself declined. Anthropologist Gayle Rubin writes:

> One of the most conspicuous features of kinship is that it has been systematically stripped of its functions—political, economic, educational. It has been reduced to its barest bones —sex and gender.
>
> The organization of sex and gender once had functions other than itself—it organized society. Now it only organizes and reproduces itself.[1]

In Western civilization, the narrowing of kinship to the nuclear family is first visible in the fourteenth century with the appearance of a new concept of childhood. According to social historian Philippe Ariès, a perceptible moral shift occurred from the view of the child as object to that of the child as subject. First witnessed in women and their coddling attitude toward children, this current had expanded by the seventeenth century into an active social interest in the psychological and moral health of the child. In turn, this interest reflected a developing focus on the "moral" individual brought on by the Protestant Reformation and the stirrings of capitalism.[2]

50 The material base for the concept of childhood was the breakdown of the manor and its serf system and the rise of smaller units of independent producers. Between the fourteenth and seventeenth centuries, while the concepts of childhood were developing, peasants and their families had their feudal ties severed, becoming tenants or landowners. With the appearance of the early bourgeoisie and the commercialization of agriculture, the manor declined. Small-scale commodity production gave birth to a class of producers working their own property.[3] Although the bourgeoisie also contained landed nobility and merchant capitalists, it was the class of producers which distinguished the family on the basis of private property and an emerging individualism. One manifestation of this individualism was the increasing concern for the child within a larger concern for privacy and a more isolated family unit.

As private property—of one's soul and one's land—became the basis for a new ideology and a new form of family, productive activity, emotional expression, and even sexuality were increasingly embraced as proper, indeed, enjoyable qualities of earthly life. Where once they had been scorned, these qualities came into their own as desirable and healthy. Since the family expressed and protected these qualities, it too rose in status. Purpose and meaning were now focused on the family and production. The secular world, torn from the rule of the spiritual, incorporated religion into its daily life as the justification for mundane pursuits. As Max Weber has demonstrated, the Protestant ethic sanctified labor, thereby facilitating the rise of capitalism. The new moral value of production lent great impetus to its spread.[4]

While complex forces narrowed the family to a nuclear unit, they also strengthened preexisting patriarchal aspects of internal power relationships within the family. Family historian Lawrence Stone remarks that the reinforcement of the father/husband's authority occurred because "the nuclear family became more free from interference by the kin, especially the wife's kin, and . . . because of wider religious, legal, and political changes which enhanced the powers of the head of the household."[5]

During the sixteenth and early seventeenth centuries in England, a besieged but authoritarian state reinforced an authoritarian family. Fortunately, this period appears to have been a temporary transition stage between the financially bonded, kin and community-oriented family of the later Middle Ages, and the affectively bonded, private and domestic-oriented family of the eighteenth century. This family had moved away from the authoritarian relationships of the transition period toward greater freedom for children, including their development as a separate status group, and more equality between spouses. Ariès notes the correlation between the development of a new emotional relationship among parents and children and the evolution of the family as a domestic unit.[6] The growth of what Stone has called "affective individualism" as a characteristic of the family attested to the progress of private life. Even the construction of houses with specialized "bedrooms" and common living spaces ("living rooms") reflected the developing desire for individual privacy. In summarizing this shift, Ariès has stated that "in the 18th century, the family began to hold society at a distance, to push it back beyond a steadily extending zone of private life."[7]

In colonial America, the family was considered a little church or commonwealth. Indeed, the interconnected, continuous nature of the family's relationship to the larger society has led at least one historian to characterize early American family relations as "the family as community."[8] But the eighteenth century American family became, like its European counterpart, a separate entity, distinct from society. By the nineteenth century, the American family had become a refuge, its crucial function a protective one.

The key to this change in the family, to an increasing emphasis on the individual and the nuclear unit as separate from the collective, is the rise of capitalism. While the impulses to a narrowing conjugal family grounded in affective bonds were present, as Stone demonstrates, centuries before the rise of capitalism, it is the removal of productive labor from the family which finally and clearly separates the family from society. More than this, it is the spirit of capitalism even prior to the onslaught of industrialization which gives the family its image, if not reality, as a refuge.[9]

The argument that capitalism split the family off from the economy, taking productive labor into factories, offices, mills, and elsewhere, is a common one. Philippe Ariès, John Demos,

51

and Lawrence Stone are among the historians who have noted this effect.[10] Because capitalism took production out of the home, a division developed between commodity production and private labor within the home. This split meant, in Demos's words, "that family life was wrenched apart from the world of work—a veritable sea-change in social history."[11]

52

This wrenching apart created an ambiguous economic position for the family, which was quickly characterized, at least in the United States, as a retreat or refuge. This new ideology, according to sociologist Arlene Skolnick, "filled the void by idealizing the home and the woman's role in it. Many of our traditional notions about femininity and family life were emphasized by industrialization: the idea that woman's place is in the home; the idea that the essence of femininity lies in ministering to the personal and psychological needs of husbands and children; the idea that mothers have a Pygmalian-like influence on their children."[12]

The developing ideology of domesticity, including the cults of the child and true womanhood, obscured the loss of women's productive status due to the seeming divorce of the family from the economy.[13] While women continued to work in cottage industries and later in factories and mills, the bourgeois ideal of the "feminine woman at home" caring for children and husband became the prevailing "sentimental model" of the nineteenth century. This ideology encouraged the division of the world into men's and women's spheres, characterizing the former as competitive and tough, the latter as revitalizing and soft.[14]

Whereas men's sphere was increasingly defined as one organized around what historian E. P. Thompson has called "time-discipline" (as required by the new capitalist industrial order), women's sphere retained the "task-orientation" that had previously been characteristic of both sexes under agricultural/artisanal economies. Under a traditional pattern of task-orientation, "social intercourse and labour are intermingled," as Thompson puts it, "the working day lengthens or contracts according to the task—and there is no great sense of conflict between labour and 'passing the time of day.'" This is precisely the opposite of industrial time-discipline, and eventually the system of task-orientation came to be considered "wasteful and lacking in urgency." Task-oriented work was thus steadily devalued, and as Thompson acknowledges, child care is the "most task-oriented of all" the family's chores.[15]

As Eli Zaretsky has pointed out, "The bourgeois familial

ideal obscured two contradictions that emerged in the course of capitalist development: the oppression of women and the family's subordination to class relations."[16] Thus, for example, while the dominant social ideal praised the wife/mother at home, her actual domestic labor was not regarded as productive. Such work was considered "natural" or "special," and therefore not in need of remuneration, or serious valuation. In a society where work came to be defined by money, any labor outside a money economy was not valued equally with wage work. Although women's work within the family was (and is) absolutely vital to the maintenance of the labor force and the socialization of children, the "naturalization" of this labor prevented due recognition while hiding women's psychological oppression and economic exploitation. With the pervasive ideology of domesticity, women's labor within the home became a "sacred mission" and, later, a professional "career."[17]

53

Beyond the economic exploitation of women, the bourgeois ideal of the family transformed precapitalist ideals of courtly love and male supremacy into ideals of romantic love and complementarity between the sexes. Marriage became a partnership in love and common destiny. However, this change in ideals, while reflecting a new direction in the ideology of women's oppression, was really an index of middle-class influence. Although the brutality of women's sixteenth-century status was softened by the development of these ideals, the evolution of male supremacy into romantic love brought a different, more insidious because more disguised form of oppression for women. On romantic and courtly love, Kate Millett has written:

> Both have had the effect of obscuring the patriarchal character of Western culture and, in their general tendency to attribute impossible virtues to women, have ended by confining them in a narrow and often remarkably conscribing sphere of behavior.
>
> The concept of romantic love affords a means of emotional manipulation which the male is free to exploit, since love is the only circumstance in which the female is (ideologically) pardoned for sexual activity. . . . Romantic love also obscures the realities of female status and the burden of economic dependency.[18]

In the modern family, the rise of individualism and the separation of family from economy have meant an increasing emphasis on personal life which historians and sociologists of the family have duly noted. But this emphasis has brought a different oppression for women who are made to appear, in their domestic capacities, perfectly suited to the new realm of subjectivity. Zaretsky summarizes this intertwining development of the nuclear family and the changed nature of women's responsibility:

54

> . . . the rise of industrial capitalism . . . gave rise to a new search for personal identity which takes place outside the division of labor. In a phrase: proletarianization gave rise to subjectivity. Many distinctively modern trends from the "child-centered" family to romantic art to an emphasis on sexuality all reflect this development. While the rise of industry largely freed women from traditional patriarchal constraints, the expansion of personal life created a new basis for their oppression—the responsibility for maintaining a private refuge from an impersonal society.[19]

Under advanced industrial capitalism, the apparent split between family and economy has been experienced by the individual as a split between "life" and "work." In anthropological terms, extended kinship relations which had joined productive labor to subjective experience and had brought the individual a "communal" rather than a "private" existence dissolved under the impact of capitalism. With the decline of communal relationships came the tightening interactions of the conjugal unit. The bourgeois family (reduced to the preservation of property) and the proletarian family (reduced to the reproduction of the labor force) both began to concentrate their increasing leisure time on a search for personal fulfillment. The intensity and pervasiveness of this search culminates in psychoanalysis—the logical result of increasing self-consciousness and its focus on childhood.[20]

Because subjectivity and the value of the "autonomous" self have attained such dignity, the family is reinforced even while capitalism and the psychodynamics of the family constantly threaten to destroy it. Despite its trauma, the family persists as the main area of an individual's personal life. Feminist historian Sheila Rowbotham says of the family:

> [It is] a place of sanctuary for all the hunted, jaded, exhausted sentiments out of place in commodity production. Chased out of the dominant mode of production where there is no room for emotion, such characteristics as love, tenderness and compassion assume a mawkish guise from confinement.

The family is thus in one sense the dummy ideal, the repository of ghostly substitutes, emotional fictions which dissolve into cloying sentimentality, or explode into thrashing, battering remorseless violence.

But this distortion of human relations still represents the only possibility of personal life. The family is the only place where human beings find whatever continuing love, security, and comfort they know. In an unloving, insecure, and comfortless society, not surprisingly people value this aspect of the family even if they rebel against the enclosing and twisting characteristics which are inherent in the intensity of the nuclear family unit.[21]

In the United States, one obvious effect of bourgeois ideology and the discontinuity between family and economy has been a concentration of meaning within the self. Because the sphere of "work" is fragmented, bureaucratic, and painfully impersonal, the estranged individual intensifies the search for meaning through drug cultures, therapy, and sexuality. While none of these can do more than temporarily alleviate what are really the effects of a grossly repressive civilization, the sense of loss and confusion is often so severe that the search for self-fulfillment is magnified. In both men and women, the quest for fulfillment often centers on each other. One explanation for the emergence of sex clinics, manuals, and movies as part of the American cultural scene is an increased feeling of chaos and alienation and a subsequent concentration of meaning in the most intimate of human acts. Sexuality and sexual relations are thus charged with a significance at once "personal" yet "social."

In the absence of political movements which fuse an analysis of alienating *work* with an analysis of unfulfilled *life*, smaller movements—mystical, social, environmental—arise in response to the degradation of "life." Although important, these movements often leave unsolved the prior reality of the split between "life" and "work." As personal life itself becomes paradoxical and confusing, the world seems more and more schizophrenic, incapable of harmony, order, unity.[22] In many critiques, madness, breakdowns, and violence are seen as rational responses to an oppressive system. Thanatos appears preferable, almost positive, where Eros has been terribly deformed.

Women and Their Role Within the Family

The place of women in this chaotic world rests at the repressive core of the dialectic of civilization. From Freud and Marcuse, we understand the organization of the sex instincts as progressively in the service of the death instincts. Anthropologists teach us of the oppressive features of this organization: male social authority, more stringent controls on female sexuality, independent personality traits in men as part of the asymmetrical gendering process, enforced heterosexuality for greater male enjoyment.

As social systems evolve into the capitalist stage, kinship declines while separation of the family from the economy follows on the increase of large-scale production and the rise of towns. Women's roles within the family, as in commodity production, are shaped by the rate of industrialization and precapitalist forms of kinship. Culture continues to affect the valuation and nature of women's work, but the essential relationship between men and women remains one of domination. Within the family, this domination can be lightened by concern and protection even while the nature of women's work is obscured or misunderstood. When women enter the market, they share all the forms of alienation and exploitation that men experience, in addition to special discrimination, hostility, and devaluation because they are women.

Meanwhile, women's "naturalization" within the "naturalized" sphere of "personal" life doubly conceals the material base under patriarchy's historical ideology of women as erotic-reproductive objects. The devaluing of women's work in the home is understood in conjunction with the devaluing of material production (which women perform) as no longer integral to commodity production. The responsibility of women for the "emotional" life of the family is but another instance of the sexual division of labor within the split between the family and the economy. Women's responsibility for "personal" life deepens the gap in the family's sexual division of labor, just as their confinement to service sectors deepens the market's division of labor. As extensions of anthropology's insights regarding domestic and public realms, the historical account of the division between "life" and "work" links women's specific oppression with the culture of everyday life. Finally, the subjectivity which marks the modern age has fallen most heavily on women. Eli Zaretsky notes:

No group experienced the subjective isolation of personal life so deeply as women, trapped as they were within the family, blamed for its egregious faults, or forced to negotiate the limbo between it and the world of wage-labor. As housewives, and particularly as mothers, women became a focus of the modern aspiration for personal happiness. The newly emerged areas of personal life were the housewife's responsibility—in particular, childhood but also sexuality, emotional expression, and the family's pattern of consumption. Far from being a refuge for women, the family was a workplace.[23]

Under advanced capitalism, women's socialization has been suited to the demands of a system where "life" needs are distinguished from "work" needs. The consciousness of women is thus greatly influenced toward the embrace of housework, child-rearing, and emotional sustenance of men and children as natural and desirable. The bourgeois ideal of the mother-wife at home remains the goal for most women in capitalist countries, despite the increasing appearance of women in the marketplace.[24] But the availability of contraception, education, and work-saving technology for the home constantly threatens this ideal by increasing the housewife's leisure time. Part of this time is filled with repetition of already accomplished tasks, that is, women "make work" for themselves. Bathrooms, kitchens, and bedrooms are redecorated, recleaned, rearranged. Increased concentration on the psychological health and development of children, although fewer and fewer in number, also takes up time. At a certain income level, consumption patterns become differentiated by a focus on useless objects. Finally, hobbies, self-development courses, and volunteer work appear as salvation for the bored and restless.[25]

The failure of the middle-class ideal is reflected in what Betty Friedan called the "problem with no name"—a sense of emptiness despite material comfort, a husband, and children.[26] This problem derives, in part, from the collapse of women's *work* into their *life*. In a situation where "work" and "life" are separated by the development of capitalism, a fusion of these two creates contradictions often painfully experienced but little recognized. *The economic marginality of women's work affects the emotional quality of their lives.* A new form of alienation is born from the contradiction between the absolute necessity of women's home production and their emotional reproduction of the labor force, and the absolute devaluation of this work. Sheila Rowbotham argues:

The non-recognition of women's labor in the home leaves them with no sense of value as a group at all. The subordination of women as a group and the particular nature of female conditioning serve to maintain this.

[A kind of] neurosis of nothingness comes directly from the nature of women's work in the home. Self-affirmation can only come through self-abnegation. The "feminine" woman, the good mother, can only realize herself by pouring herself into her husband and children. She has to give herself in service and find herself through other people and through the objects around her in the house.[27]

Because women's production in the home has been seen as their "life," when women actually work in the market, their domestic duties are still considered primary. Therefore, the structure and organization of the market, despite the expansion of production, segregates jobs according to cultural standards of women's and men's "work." The inequality of woman at work is illustrated by the sexual division of labor and the devaluation of women's work, and by discrimination in pay, promotion, and benefits. The ideology of "woman's place" keeps women in service-oriented jobs, out of competition with men, and away from top positions of power in all fields—scientific, industrial, commercial, political, legal, even educational.[28]

Both in their market labor and in their home production, women are subject to the strains of living in a system which divides "life" from "work" but forces women to mediate between the two. Housework is an excellent example. By its nonspecialized nature and isolation, housework belies categorization. At once a combination of many low-paid jobs—waitress, maid, chauffeur, cook, babysitter—housework also brings certain advantages which such jobs lack: flexible schedules, relative autonomy, a privatized, personalized character. Because housework is a ministration to other's needs, emotion and intimate considerations constantly break the day's routine, fragmenting concentration and the flow of tasks. Thus a woman's mind is filled with trivial detail and the management of drudgery, or is inundated by the deepest crises of her family's individual lives.

Childrearing, while often combined with housework, is quite different. Meaningful and significant because it deals with a growing, impressionable human being, childrearing has become both less taxing and more demanding. Schools and nurseries free women from many basic tasks associated with the constant care of children, but the rise of self-consciousness almost to a point of fetishism has brought new demands on women as mothers. More and more, women are judged responsible for the mental and emotional well-being of their children. Despite the reality of an increasingly complex, mobile society, women are still expected to raise good, obedient citizens. Failures in the child, then, are failures in the mother. Even with a growing awareness of the power of education, youth culture, and social trends to shape the minds and actions of children and adolescents, mothers remain the primary socializing forces in society's ideology.[29]

The responsibility of women for the maturity and capacities of their children is part of the family's role in socializing the young to fit into an alienating society. While the father's role as authority figure is eroded daily by the penetration of large organizations into the life of the family, the mother's role becomes conservative and increasingly subject to strain. In an unloving, often cruel world, mothers are expected to remain fountains of affection, self-sacrifice, and peace. As wives, women are expected to provide the meaning and purpose which the world of "work" denies their husbands. Sheila Rowbotham writes:

> The family as a place of retreat and sexuality as a means of release become increasingly important as compensatory ideals as capitalism makes both retreat and release impossible within the world of work.
>
> The condition of the preservation of the "ideal" family as of the "ideal" fuck are definitions of female nature which are not only imposed, but imposed in order to maintain the interest men have in finding compensation from the exploitation and alienation capitalism forces on them at work.[30]

Rowbotham suggests that the particular exploitations of capitalism create new forms of oppression for women. In crude terms, the more alienating and exploitative the world of "work," the more idealized the world of "life." Given women's traditional responsibilities for nurturance, this means even greater reliance on their mothering capacities. Historically, as Zaretsky points out, these expectations arise just at a time when "personal" life and subjectivity have increased meaning for increased numbers of people. Moreover, the development of the middle-class family has meant women's increased concentration on childrearing. One result of this focus is an expanded emphasis on an individual's psychological and emotional well-being, that is, on the quality of "personal" life. The irony of capitalism (or its dialectic) seems to be that as exploitation and alienation increase, so does the focus on "personal" meaning. Put another way, the individual under capitalism suffers a peculiar kind of alienation just when the potential for personal life is historically at its greatest point. This may partly explain why large numbers of women, weary of bearing the emotional brunt of capitalism, have begun to identify with the analysis and aspirations of feminism.

Rowbotham's point about the increasing importance of sexuality as a compensatory ideal also means an increased emphasis on women's erotic capacities. Not only does capitalism demand more of women's nurturant qualities, it also means larger and different kinds of expectations and exploitations of women's sexual capacity. Men's dominant cultural position has resulted in men's dominance in sexual relations, their demand for sexual gratification and their disregard for women's gratification, and a double standard of sexual morality.[31] But as sensitivity to women's sexual capacity increases and as sexual preferences are regarded with more flexibility (the so-called "sexual revolution"), the heritage of men's hegemony reaches down into the most intimate of communications between men and women. This is one explanation behind the feminist concept of the personal as the political. In our time, the most personal of experiences, the orgasm, has become the most public of subjects. With the advent of women's liberation, the orgasm as an indication of sexual politics has moved to center stage.[32]

The concentration of meaning and conflict in sexuality has served many ends. With advertising, women's objectification has attained monstrous proportions. Capitalism's dependence on increasing consumption has forced commodification of the most personal attributes. The "sexual sell" accompanies new products, new policies, new people.[33] Because of her historic characterization as erotic, woman is easy prey to this slickest of exploitations. Within the so-called "sexual revolution" women are given new freedoms by virtue of contraception and changing sexual mores, but they are under pressures to separate sexual relations from emotional commitment, thereby joining in a cool promiscuity. Finally, sexuality carries an overloaded quality. Representing the desire for a protective, generous alternative in a violent society, sex becomes the explosive focus of denied and deformed drives. Excitement is polluted by fantasies of abuse too real in everyday life. Affection is burdened by game-playing, rituals of a false courtship endlessly exploited in social manners and cultural artifacts from cinema to literature. Need is perceived as weakness or sickness in a universe of manipulated needs. And concern, like joy, is made brief by the demands of compartmentalized time. If men find this condition oppressive, women, as the instinctual and historical source of gratification, find it even more destructive—for men, no matter what their class, retain the culturally sanctioned power to use and abuse women sexually, psychologically, and emotionally.

If the line between sexual expression and exploitation is a vague one in interpersonal relationships, the division between emotional nurturance and emotional abuse is no less troubling. The positive value of women's capacity to nurture, to care for and with another human being in an intimate way, is often abused by the prevailing belief that such sustenance is natural, requiring no nurturance of its own. Women are caught by their desire and capacity to "give" precisely because men are not psychologically and emotionally equipped to reciprocate.

When progressively accustomed to emotional exploitation by men and children, women often embrace daily self-sacrifice as an unfolding of their true identity. Reinforced by gender identity and confined by cultural ideology, law, and custom, such "victim" psychology appears the norm of "femininity." It was this kind of "femininity" which Freud described and approved. As a deformation of the instinct to encourage and protect life (Eros), this self-sacrificing ethic is both reality and symbol of "feminine" masochism.

In the ontology of relationships, men reflect the complement of feminine masochism—masculine sadism. Their constant reliance on women's nurturance encourages an exploitative psyche, crippling men's emotional capacities both to feel and to give. The resulting "psychological backwardness" of men—their silences, escapes, and flights into violence in the face of relational strain—is the familiar counter to women's abused and neglected sensitivities. Both sexes are fitted to the "normal" but destructive pattern: women are chained by nurturance, men by their deformed need of it. Supported by cultural images of victimization—for example, rape as the expression of virility; physical-psychological violation as women's secret, fulfilling desire (Freud's basic argument)—masculine sadism and feminine masochism reveal the trauma of a wounded Eros.

Given the global development of capitalism and its effects, the family's discontinuity with the economy appears certain.

While different societies will transmit their particular cultural form of sexual politics from generation to generation, the devaluation and subordination of women will change only in its specifics, not in its universals. An increase in consumer goods, leisure time, privacy, and subjectivity will specify new forms of oppression rather than an end to them. In the developing world (including the island nations of the Pacific), increased economic dependence on larger industrial core nations (Europe, Japan, the United States) will force indigenous and Third World peoples into worsening conditions of bondage. For women, this means all the exploitation inherent in dependency alongside an assumed sexual subjugation, for as long as the sexual understructure remains, whether concentrated in the nuclear unit or some other form of the family, women's specific oppression will continue. If the experience in advanced industrial nations and their satellite dependents is any indication, capitalism will result in new deformations of women's condition.

Notes

1. Gayle Rubin, "The Traffic in Women," in *Toward an Anthropology of Women*, ed. Rayna Reiter (New York: Monthly Review Press, 1975), p. 199.

2. Phillipe Ariès, *Centuries of Childhood: A Social History of Family Life*, trans. Robert Baldick (New York: Alfred A. Knopf, 1962), p. 128.

3. Barrington Moore Jr., *Social Origins of Dictatorship and Democracy* (Boston: Beacon, 1966), pp. 20–29.

4. Max Weber, *The Protestant Ethic and the Spirit of Capitalism*, trans. Talcott Parsons (New York: Scribner, 1958).

5. Lawrence Stone, *The Family, Sex, and Marriage in England 1500–1800* (New York: Harper and Row, 1977), p. 124.

6. Ariès, *Centuries of Childhood*, p. 398.

7. Ibid.

8. John Demos, "Images of the American Family, Then and Now," in *Changing Images of the Family*, ed. Virginia Tufte and Barbara Myerhoff (New Haven: Yale University Press, 1979), pp. 43–60.

9. Ibid. See also, Arlene Skolnick, "Public Images, Private Realities: The American Family in Popular Culture and Social Science," in *Changing Images of the Family*, pp. 297–315.

10. See Ariès, *Centuries of Childhood*; Demos, "Images of the American Family"; and Stone, *The Family, Sex, and Marriage*.

11. Demos, "Images of the American Family," p. 52.

12. Skolnick, "Public Images, Private Realities," p. 304.

13. Barbara Welter, "The Cult of True Womanhood: 1820–1860," in *The American Family in Social Historical Perspective*, ed. Michael Gordon (New York: St. Martin's Press, 1973), pp. 224–250. On the emergence of the cult of childhood, see also Bernard Wishy, *The Child and the Republic: The Dawn of Modern American Child Nurture* (Philadelphia: University of Pennsylvania Press, 1968).

14. Skolnick, "Public Images, Private Realities," pp. 305–306.

15. E. P. Thompson, "Time, Work-Discipline, and Industrial Capitalism," *Past and Present*, 38 (1967): 56–79.

16. Eli Zaretsky, *Capitalism, the Family and Personal Life* (New York: Harper, 1976), pp. 33–34.

17. Skolnick, "Public Images, Private Realities," pp. 305–306.

18. Kate Millett, *Sexual Politics* (New York: Avon, 1971), p. 37; cf. Jean-Louis Flandrin's comment that "according to the confessors of the nineteenth century, the blows to which peasant women were accustomed might be less hard to endure than the cruelties of bourgeois husbands." *Families in Former Times* (Cambridge: Cambridge University Press, 1979), p. 123.

19. Zaretsky, *Capitalism, the Family, and Personal Life*, pp. 9–10.

20. For some discussion of this and related matters, see Jacques Donzelot, *The Policing of Families* (New York: Pantheon, 1979); and Michel Foucault, *The History of Sexuality* (New York: Pantheon, 1979), esp. pp. 112–113, 129–131.

21. Sheila Rowbotham, *Woman's Consciousness, Man's World* (Middlesex, Eng.: Penguin Books, 1973), p. 59. For further historical background on this in the United States, see Christopher Lasch, *Haven in a Heartless World* (New York: Basic Books, 1977). For similar developments in modern France, see Donzelot, *The Policing of Families*.

22. Zaretsky, *Capitalism, the Family, and Personal Life*, pp. 118–123.

23. Ibid., p. 113.

24. See, e.g., William H. Chafe, *The American Woman: Her Changing Social, Economic, and Political Role, 1920–1970* (New York: Oxford University Press, 1972); Edith Hoshino Altbach, ed., *From Feminism to Liberation* (Cambridge, Mass.: Schenkman Publishing Co., 1971); Juanita Kreps, *Sex in the Marketplace: American Women at Work* (Baltimore: Johns Hopkins University Press, 1971).

25. See Betty Freidan, *The Feminine Mystique* (New York: Dell, 1963).

63

26. Ibid., pp. 11–25.

27. Rowbotham, *Woman's Consciousness, Man's World*, p. 76.

28. See Chafe, *The American Woman*, and Kreps, *Sex in the Marketplace*.

64

29. See Edith Hoshino Altbach, *Women in America* (Lexington, Mass.: D. C. Heath, 1974). Cf. Donzelot, *The Policing of Families*, esp. pp. 217–229. On household work, see Ann Oakeley, *The Sociology of Housework* (New York: Pantheon, 1974); Margaret Benston, "The Political Economy of Women's Liberation," in Altbach, *Women in America*, pp. 199–209; and Meredith Tax, *Woman and Her Mind: The Story of Daily Life* (Cambridge, Mass.: Bread and Roses, 1970).

30. Rowbotham, *Woman's Consciousness, Man's World*, p. 53.

31. See, e.g., women's complaints about men, and their feelings of neglect because of male selfishness regarding female gratification; Shere Hite, *The Hite Report* (New York: Dell, 1976).

32. Ibid. See also Mary Jane Sherfey, *The Nature and Evolution of Female Sexuality* (New York: Vintage Books, 1973); Lonnie Barbach, *For Yourself* (New York: Dell, 1978).

33. See, among many analyses of this, John Berger, *Ways of Seeing* (London: Pelican, 1975); Erving Goffman, *Gender Advertisements* (Cambridge, Mass.: Harvard University Press, 1979); and Joan Mellen, *Women and Their Sexuality in the New Film* (New York: Dell, 1973).

Four · Psychology

If women's subordination in the West is intimately tied to their oppression within the family, then an understanding of the family is essential for understanding the oppression of women.

Mothering and the Sexual Division of Labor

Many feminists have noted that a major structural feature of patriarchy is the hierarchic division between public and private spheres of social organization. The private, domestic sphere is characterized by relational ties naturalized on the basis of biology. Women and children form the domestic unit. Because women are responsible for child care, their primary social location is domestic. Although men have domestic, relational ties, their primary location is in the public sphere. Here, relations are determined by social rather than biological criteria: institutions develop according to rules which transcend the particularistic and biological, thereby establishing the "cultural." Through men's location in the public realm, culture and society come to be defined as male, as masculine. Social and political power accrues to men, including control over women's erotic-reproductive capacities. The public sphere dominates the domestic, men dominate women. Sociologist Nancy Chodorow says:

> A sexual division of labor in which women mother organizes babies and separates domestic and public spheres. Heterosexual marriage, which usually gives men rights in women's sexual and reproductive capacities and formal rights in children, organizes sex. Both together organize and reproduce gender as an unequal social relation.[1]

Women's mothering capacity is primarily psychological, despite its grounding in women's biology. The ability to establish an intimate, ongoing, affective relationship with an infant constitutes mothering, and could be done by men as well as women. The basic ingredient is the quality and constancy of love and care, not the sex of the loving parent. That women rather than men have been the primary caretakers of children is thus a product of the organization of sex and gender, that is, of history rather than biology.

66   The Psychoanalytic Perspective

As a body of knowledge with its own principles and methodology, psychoanalytic theory has accompanied the rise of subjectivity and the focus on the individual. It offers rich perspectives on the engendering of the "sexual understructure" because it is essentially a theory of the family. Of course, much of psychoanalytic theory, following Freud, has been patriarchal in its analysis and recommendations. But the Women's Movement has produced a group of feminist theorists whose work offers a counterbalance to this traditional emphasis.

One of the best among these theorists is Nancy Chodorow. While her work is unquestionably controversial, it nevertheless remains a useful tool for exploring the psychodynamics of the family, particularly women's mothering.[2]

Chodorow, like others, relies on a psychoanalytic account because it helps to explain how the Western family is reproduced, how infants develop from a pre-Oedipal phase, where the mother and issues of primary love and identification are overriding, to an Oedipal phase, where the father and issues of sex and gender are paramount. The experiences of the female child and the male child are different in these phases, and continue to be different throughout the latency, prepuberty, and adolescent stages. These differences account for several gender/personality developments, such as greater relational capacities in women than men. They also explain why women find gratification in mothering and men do not. When linked to the larger domestic/public dichotomy, the engendering of women's mothering capacity illuminates the whole process of social reproduction, including the sexual sociology of adult life.

Chodorow's Psychoanalytic Account

In the mother-child-father triangle, the mother is far more significant in the early years of the child's development than the father. Because she is primary caretaker, the mother establishes a bond with the child which becomes the prototype for later relationships. Her care and interaction shape the child's sense of self and direct the child's needs and gratifications.

Originally, children of both sexes are matrisexual. The girl experiences a longer pre-Oedipal relationship to her mother, which means a prolonged involvement with issues of individuation and an attachment characterized by primary identification. The boy is pushed out of the pre-Oedipal period by his mother and experiences a sudden curtailment of his fusion with her. He is forced to deal with and resolve individual issues. Because of the girl's longer pre-Oedipal experience, "relational qualities" become a basic part of her primary definition of self. In addition, boys tend to deny relational modes even while they continue to need them.

In the Oedipal period, girls experience penis envy as a result of the superior valuation of male genitals, and as a result of the impact of this valuation on an ambivalent desire both to possess and yet be free from the mother. The boy's fear of castration by the father causes repression of love for the mother. Since both children are originally involved with the mother, only the girl has to achieve a change of object (to the father) in order to attain heterosexuality. The boy's major Oedipal goal is masculine identification with the father achieved through superego formation and the disparagement of women.

Chodorow argues, against traditional psychoanalytic theory, that the significance of the Oedipal period is not in the development of gender identity or heterosexual orientation, but in the development of "relational potential" in boys and girls. In the Oedipal period, a girl does not give up or repress her mother for her father, but adds love for him to her world of primary objects. Chodorow argues that the girl defines herself in a relational triangle; this triangle is imposed upon another inner triangle which involves a girl's internal Oedipal and pre-Oedipal mother. Therefore, there is greater complexity in the feminine inner object world than in the masculine.

What this means is that there is a developmental distinction between genital heterosexuality and heterosexual love. Girls generally become genitally heterosexual but retain a strong emotional attachment to other women (including their mothers). Depending on the quality of the relationship with the father, with the mother, and between father and mother, men often become emotionally secondary to women, even while heterosexual orientation is the feminine norm. This compares to the Oedipal boy's emotional tie to women, which he must repress if he is to achieve masculine identity. In his adolescence, the boy is expected to move toward his birthright—a woman (compensation for the mother) and a place of cultural privilege. However, his attainment of masculinity is often insecure because it is based on idealized role identification rather than on an immediate relationship with the father. Constant reiteration of a man's privilege, and his ownership of and scorn for women, are often a result of this insecurity. (Such behavior can also be traced to fear of the omnipotent mother.)[3]

Because of women's mothering, then, the relational experiences of boys and girls are asymmetrical, which accounts for crucial differences in feminine and masculine personalities and their relational modes. Chodorow argues:

> From the retention of preoedipal attachments to their mother, growing girls come to define and experience themselves as continuous with others; their experience of self contains more flexible or permeable ego boundaries. Boys come to define themselves as more separate and distinct, with a greater sense of rigid ego boundaries. . . . The basic feminine sense of self is connected to the world, the basic masculine sense of self is separate.
>
> Masculine personality, then, comes to be defined more in terms of denial of relation and connection (and denial of femininity), whereas feminine personality comes to include a fundamental definition of self in relationship. Thus, relational abilities and preoccupations have been extended in women's development and curtailed in men's.[4]

Gender Identification and Gender Role Training

Relational capacities, like a sense of self, are defining characteristics of personality. We have seen how the asymmetrical organization of parenting, specifically women's mothering, has directly structured the development of pre-Oedipal and Oedipal stages to produce "feminine" and "masculine" personalities.

These gender categories are reinforced even when boys' and girls' socialization is similar, and when both sexes can participate in extrafamilial institutions: the worlds of business, education, arts, and sciences. The process of gender identification and reinforcement in the child's later development has already been prepared by a sexual division of labor which grounds femininity in mothering and the family, and masculinity in nonfamilial activities in the public world. Women's mothering begins the gendering process and reproduces it in the next generation. Culture and ideology, with women's mothering as justification, separate domestic from public spheres. Personality is developed in relation to these domains—women will find their primary location in the family; men will find their primary location in the public world. Therefore, femininity will entail familial characteristics—affective, diffuse obligations—and masculinity will entail nonfamilial characteristics—abstract qualities, repression of affective relationships.

In learning their gender, little girls identify with their mother, a process which continues the primary tie. The girl learns from her mother all the attributes of being a woman; she internalizes and comes to feel much of what her mother feels. Such an intimate identification with someone's behavior and personality is called "personal" identification. Children apparently prefer this type of relationship because it is close, immediate, and real.

"Positional" identification, by contrast, is based on abstracted aspects of roles rather than an ongoing, intimate relationship with someone. This kind of identification is prone to idealization because a concrete example is often lacking.

In father-absent families within patriarchal society, the primary caretaking role of the mother means that a girl's identification is embedded in her relationship with her mother. Such "personal" identification encourages a "feminine" personality based on relations with other people. The boy, meanwhile, experiences a "positional" identification with the "masculine" role, that is, frequent absence of his father and the overpowering presence of his mother force the boy to identify with specific aspects of his father's masculinity (rather than with his father as a total personality). The boy often learns what it is to be a "man" through cultural definitions.

For both boys and girls, development of gender identity can be difficult. The problems each faces, however, are different. Girls may experience confusion and an inability to become separate individuals because their identification processes are so embedded in an immediate relationship. Boys may remain insecure about their "masculinity" because it is partially based on stereotypes and on the internalization of aspects of their father's personality which are feared. In addition, "masculinity" is defined as much negatively as it is positively. Given cultural definitions of "femininity" as opposite and inferior to "masculinity," and given the omniscient force of the mother, a young boy comes to identify masculinity as that which is not feminine and, later, as that which is not domestic.

Paradoxically for both boys and girls, mother comes to represent regression and a lack of autonomy. For girls, the contradiction between mother-identification and self-definition threatens to become a lifelong problem. For boys, mother and all she represents—dependency, attachment, and nurturance—are antithetical to masculinity. These "feminine" qualities must be denied and devalued if a boy is to "be a man."

Like the post-Oedipal replay, the gender identification process encourages women to define themselves in particularistic, affective, personal ways, while encouraging men to define themselves in abstract, categorical ways which tend to deny affection and relationship.

Gender Personality and Society

Women's roles within the family and within society draw on diffuse personal and emotional qualities of interaction, qualities comprising a kind of "femininity" represented in the mother-infant bond. Anthropologists believe that characterization to be universal. Everywhere, women's roles are more personal than cultural, more immediate than institutional. The power which women do exercise is often expressed through personal channels, especially since institutional power is generally denied them. In crossing groups, and mediating within the family and between the family and the larger social world, women are performing their translating functions (socializer, mother, actual and symbolic nurturer), between nature and culture.

While women's personality is molded for the domestic sphere and extensions thereof (teachers, nursers, service workers), men's personality is fitted to the demands of the public sphere. Under advanced capitalism, within bureaucracy and hierarchy, the defining traits of masculinity—repression of attachment, denial of the world of women, an appropriation of the male world and masculine privilege—are suited to the demands of an alienating public domain.

Summary

Chodorow's argument, which I have presented in very abbreviated form, is this: the asymmetrical organization of parenting—women's exclusive mothering, and men's dominant but absent

family role—gives rise to the asymmetrical development of relational, affective qualities in boys and girls. Greater capacity
for relationship in girls and women is a direct result of a prolonged pre-Oedipal (mother-infant) period, and an ambivalent
Oedipal (mother-infant-father) period. Lesser relational capacity in boys and men is a direct result of a truncated pre-Oedipal
period and a traumatic, quickly resolved Oedipal period.

Both pre-Oedipal and Oedipal periods are prolonged for the
girl because the mother views her as an extension or double,
rather than as a different *other*, like the boy. The mother's perception and sexualization of her relationship with her son are a
result of living in a patriarchal society which values the male
more than the female. This sexualization pushes the son into
the Oedipal stage where sexual issues assume predominance
over separation-fusion issues (pre-Oedipal concerns). The classic Oedipal issue—castration anxiety—is a result of the unequal relationship between father and mother, men and women.
That is, the boy would not experience castration anxiety if the
mother was not possessed by the father. And the mother would
not perceive and treat her children differently if society did not
value them unequally. The mother's perception of the son, and
her relationship to him, are thus intimately connected with her
relationship to her husband and to the larger, male-dominated
society. In viewing her son as a "little man," wanting him to
be "masculine," the mother is acknowledging and transmitting
his birthright of dominance over women. The presence of the
father assures that this birthright extends only to women *other
than* the mother. In upholding the incest taboo between
mother and son, father (and society) promise the son general
male dominance.

The daughter, meanwhile, is kept closer to the mother and
thus enjoys a deepening relational capacity which will be fulfilled, in later life, only through another symbiotic relationship
(more on this in the following section). She is sexualized by the
father for her proper "feminine" role—biological and emotional
mothering. Possession of the mother by the father promises a
similar possession of the daughter by another man (not the father), a possession which is fraught with inequality in both love
and power. Surplus repression is that required by the law of
male dominance: castration anxiety and truncated relational capacity in boys to ensure accession to possession and power over
women; ambivalence within a rich relational capacity but sub-
servience to the patriarchal order in girls to ensure the con-

tinuation of women's exclusive mothering and control of their erotic/reproductive capacities by men.

The structure which ensures this surplus-repression is the asymmetrical organization of parenting within the contemporary form of Marcuse's performance principle: the nuclear family. The pre-Oedipal and Oedipal stages are the psychic story of our social heritage: *because only women mother*, they are the desired love object of both female and male children (that is, both children are matrisexual). But women, within the family and within society, *belong* to the father (patriarchy, culture). Neither son nor daughter can "possess" the mother because she is already "possessed" by the father. For men, phallic culture decrees another woman (not the mother) and domination. The prior importance of the phallus is a product of patriarchal values, and not of any biological superiority. In a patriarchal society, the phallus distinguishes the "exchanger" from the "exchanged," the powerful from the powerless. Juxtaposing psychoanalysis and anthropology, the phallus becomes the source of power through which the vagina and womb (women's erotic-reproductive personalities) are passed. In reverse, the vagina and womb are conduits for the source of power, the phallus. The circulation of the phallus in intrafamily exchange is an inversion of the circulation of women in interfamily exchange. Anthropologist Gayle Rubin contends: "[The phallus] is the embodiment of the male status, to which men accede, and in which certain rights inhere—among them, the right to a woman. It is an expression of the transmission of male dominance."[5]

The sexual understructure is built into our psychologies. From Chodorow's work, we understand how mothering becomes an institutional women's role through the unequal development of psychological capacities. Women's mothering capacity (not just their physical role, but their emotional, relational capacity) is what ties women to their young, and to their confining existence under patriarchy.

This argument about the reproduction of mothering and the engendering of "feminine" and "masculine" personalities reveals the relationship between feeling and structure to be a *symbiotic* one. Chodorow's work, in its subtlety and range, explores how psychologically binding the mother-knot can be. It also explains how men can survive in a brutal world: they exist, as emotional parasites, off women's nurturance.

The psychoanalytic approach to the creation of the sexual division of labor helps us to understand that social valuation and

72

institutional reality are not the only forces which confine women to mothering. Women's own relational needs, not merely their maternal capacities, are gratified in mothering. The creation of these needs is the result of women's exclusive mothering. How and why the gratification of these needs leads adult women back to the mothering relation is the subject of the next section.

Mothering, Heterosexuality, and Love

The patriarchal order, built on the primacy of men and masculist assumptions, naturalizes gender according to function: femininity *entails* mothering, nurturance and love, dependence; masculinity *entails* possession, denial of nurturance and attachment, independence. Men and women come to have different gender identities and needs, in great part because their original relationship to the mother is both exclusive and embedded in, saturated by, patriarchal assumptions (e.g., the superiority of male sexual needs, the cultural justification of women's nature as maternal). The mother-infant bond forms the psychological ground of our desire (conscious and unconscious) to re-create our original infant experience of symbiosis through intimate adult relationships. But relational needs are different and are satisfied differently in men and women. Chodorow argues that the most common form of this gratification (heterosexual intercourse for men, mothering for women) partly explains why women mother and how mothering is reproduced in the next generaton.

Heterosexual Orientation

If Chodorow is correct, the basic difference in relational capacity and need between men and women explains not only women's mothering but also the nature of heterosexual relationship. Chodorow suggests that the goal of adult sexual relationships (heterosexual and homosexual) is re-creation of the "primary" love between mother and infant. However, re-creation of the oneness, intimacy, and merging of primary love is more easily achieved by men than by women, allegedly because intercourse with a woman "is more completely a return to the mother." Because woman's body, her erotic nature, and her possessed flesh remind man, even if briefly, of mother-infant bliss, he is more likely to satisfy his needs for intimacy and closeness through intercourse. Woman either identifies with man's penetration of her or visualizes herself as the enveloping mother. In both instances, women's experience of merging is a vicarious one. The implication here is that the body of the loved one, rather than the emotional context in which intercourse is experienced, determines gratification of the desire for oneness. In heterosexual intercourse, it is because woman's body resembles the mother's that the man is able to relive infantile bliss while the woman is not.

Dorothy Dinnerstein has elaborated on this argument.[6] Calling the inevitable loss of primary love and infantile bliss the original, basic human grief, she theorizes that mastery, competence, and enterprise—the new joys of successful activity in compensation for the old joys of passive wish-fulfillment—are indirect consolations for "loss of mother." Direct consolations are sought in love-making. Both women and men try to re-experience the infant's role of omnipotence as well as the mother's role of nurturance in lovemaking; both *take* bodily pleasure (infant) and *provide* bodily pleasure (mother). But the exchange of pleasure, as women well know, tends to be unequal. Dinnerstein, like others, explains the inequality between men and women from a biologic perspective:

> She [woman] is the one whose physique more closely resembles the physique of the first parent, and who is likely to have incorporated this parent's attitudes more deeply; he is therefore apt to be the one who can more literally relive the infant experience of fulfilling primitive wishes through unqualified access to another body. For her, the vicarious version of this reliving—providing the body through which the other's wishes are perfectly granted—is likely to be a more prominent feature of the interplay.[7]

I would note that the idea of the goal of adult sexual relationships as an attempt to recapture primary love is based on an "emotional" argument, that is, we desire the "emotional" gratification of merging and oneness; physical merging (intercourse) is but the occasion, the medium through which we express our desire for emotional merging. But the argument as constructed by therapists, including Dinnerstein, implies a *physical* reason for differences in *emotional* gratification between women and men. It appears that a woman can more easily provide a return to the mother because her body and its penetration allow the man a return to primary love. A woman apparently has a difficult time in recreating a similar experience because a man's body, and her merging with it, do not trigger an approximation of infant bliss. While it is clear, at least in the United States, that men achieve orgasm regularly in intercourse and women do not (partly because intercourse provides direct stimulation for men and only indirect stimulation for women, but also because men tend to view intercourse as completed upon their orgasm, with little concern for women's gratification), the assumption in the above argument is based on penetration (a male paradigm in thinking about sexuality, since only men, in the cultural ideology, can penetrate). Since women cannot penetrate men physically, emotional merging is difficult without vicarious identification. It is woman's body rather than any emotional attachment which is assumed to trigger a reexperiencing of primary love.

This line of reasoning assumes the basis of primary love to be physical experience (of the mother by the infant). And indeed, much of psychoanalytic theory does assume this. However, I would argue that Chodorow's work supports our own life knowledge of primary love and its re-creation as an emotional, psychological experience rather than a predominantly physical experience. In infancy we experience ourselves as part of the mother, and she as part of us. We are not a separate entity desiring to possess the mother. During the pre-Oedipal period, the infantile ego has not formed sufficiently to distinguish between the I/not-I. Therefore, disjunction between infant needs and care produces a direct threat to the self rather than to possession of the mother. It is the desire to be wholly satisfied and loved which forms the ground of infant and adult striving and which, when achieved, bonds infant and mother, lover and loved, in primary love. Thus the satisfaction of physical need (e.g., hunger), while a prerequisite for growth, is not sufficient; only love and warmth, nurturance and care, can provide the glow of intimate oneness.

This emotional experience is qualitatively an experience of the whole being, not merely one physical aspect of being. *If* a man can more nearly re-create this emotional experience in intercourse (and it is not clear that he can, for intercourse may be more physical release than emotional merging for a man), it is because he feels loved and nurtured by the woman, not because he can penetrate and take her. Penetration is merely a physical act (although one grossly overrated in the definition of cultural "masculinity") and as such can only facilitate attainment of the "oceanic feeling," never equal it. The "return to the mother" is a return to love, something therapists, like Dinnerstein, seem to have forgotten in their rush to explain greater male gratification in heterosexual intercourse.

Following Chodorow's argument that women have greater relational capacities than men, it seems more plausible to suggest that men may be re-creating the experience of primary love more completely than women because women are providing men with nurturance and care, that is, with love. Given that "femininity" is defined in terms of nurturance and that "masculinity" is defined in terms of its denial, it is not surprising that men might achieve the sense of oneness *as themselves*, while women achieve it vicariously. Men's truncated relational capacities make it especially difficult for them to reciprocate the nurturance and caring which women provide. When coupled with men's culturally encouraged disregard for women's sexual gratification, the crucial relational gap between the sexes (rather than any physical attribute) accounts for the differential re-creation of primary love in heterosexual intercourse.

If we juxtapose the careful constructions of the best of psychoanalytic theory with the prevailing wisdom that women love more and better, and are more sensitive and caring than men, we have a clear explanation for the increasing evidence of men's chronic failure to satisfy women, orgasmically and emotionally.[8]

In other words, feminist psychoanalytic theory has fleshed out in detail the causes and influences of an everyday observation: because of the gendering process, men really are selfish, less sensitive, more egotistical; they really do receive more out of heterosexual relationships than women. Women, meanwhile, are more nurturant and solicitous, really give more in heterosexual relationships because of their gendering process.

Why so many women accept this condition of relationship is the final link in the reproduction of mothering. The increasing numbers of women who refuse to relate under such conditions are the future hope for the changing of the entire sexual understructure, particularly the asymmetrical organization of parenting.

Mothers and Children

The incompatibilities between women's and men's relational needs encourage women to look elsewhere for emotional gratification. Because men both want and fear intimacy, they find it difficult to engage women on the same level of emotional intensity. It becomes easier for men, especially when supported by patriarchal institutions and ideology, to relate to other men on the less threatening basis of abstract role-expectations. Men relate, in our culture, through common interests in sports or work or some objectively perceived category rather than as men with personal attributes and desires. Comradeship among men often entails conscious disparagement of women along with competitive interaction. Unsatisfied by the lack of relational depth in their heterosexual relationships, women then seek close ties with other women. But, the argument goes, it is children, and the re-creation of the mother-infant bond with their own child, which allows women to recapture the experience of primary love. Thus both women and men maintain an emotional distance from each other: women look to other women and children for relational gratification; men look to their work and other men for safe emotional outlets.

While most women and men express a heterosexual preference, their different relational needs create strains and contradictions in heterosexual relationships. The great extent to which these difficulties can be attributed to women's exclusive care of children has been argued in the previous chapter. Women's mothering and men's dominance create (1) complex relational needs in women, (2) the repression of affective needs in men, (3) the idealization of men and masculinity, and (4) a division between public and domestic spheres based on gender.

Despite the predominance of heterosexual preference, women and men are segregated across cultures:

> Women tend to have closer personal ties with each other than men have, and to spend more time in the company of women than they do with men. In our society, there is some evidence that women's friendships are affectively richer than men's. In other societies, and in most subcultures of our own, women remain involved with female relatives in adulthood. . . . These relationships are one way of resolving and recreating the mother-daughter bond and are an expression of women's general relational capacities and definition of self in relationship.[9]

In the United States, taboos on homosexuality, increasing isolation of women in nuclear families, and the predominance of heterosexual preference make deep affective relationships with women both difficult and scarce. Despite the recent increase in such relationships (partly a result of the Women's Movement), women's search for love and nurturance remains centered on the family.

We recall that as a result of asymmetrical parenting, women's psyche is made up of a layering of relational constellations. Emotional needs created during both the pre-Oedipal mother-child period and the Oedipal triangle continue to be important throughout women's lives. When heterosexual relationships fail to satisfy these needs, women seek gratification through a symbiotic relationship with a child of their own.

On some level, then, women's relationship to men is experienced as *incomplete* in terms of mutual caring and love. Because of this, children serve to *complete* women, fulfilling the prophecy of patriarchal ideology that mothering is women's destiny. Chodorow concludes:

> Women come to want and need primary relationships to children. These wants and needs result from wanting intense primary relationships, which men tend not to provide both because of their place in women's oedipal constellation and because of their difficulties with intimacy. Women's desires for intense primary relationships tend not to be with other women, both because of internal and external taboos on homosexuality, and because of women's isolation from their primary female kin (especially mothers) and other women.[10]

It is clear that many women *and* men come to want to have children for reasons other than the re-creation of primary love. Paramount among these is the desire, so eloquently expressed by de Beauvoir, to extend one's self beyond the bounds of this lifetime, that is, the desire for immortality. In different forms, this includes the wish to ensure the continuation of one's culture, or ethnic group, even of one's family.

Therapists do not address these larger needs and reasons for having children. We might think of these as species needs for survival rather than psychological needs for individual fulfillment. The satisfaction of both women's needs and men's needs for the re-creation of primary love in intercourse, then, would not necessarily eliminate the desire to have children. It might, however, make conception and childrearing less dependent on women's emotional dissatisfaction in heterosexual relationships.

78

Personality, Relationship, and Love: An Interpretation

In detailing the psychological and emotional development of masculine and feminine personality in Western culture, feminist psychoanalytic theory has given solid explanation to common experiences of mothering, love, and heterosexual relationship. Our personalities are not only formed in a given family environment where women have major responsibilities for child care and men are both dominant and absent, but these very personalities contribute to our difficulties in relationship, our inequalities of caring and creativity between men and women.

For women, femininity continues to mean the bondage of biological and emotional mothering. Despite real advances in the material conditions under which Western women live, self-sacrifice, truncated intellectual development, educational denial, sociopolitical ignorance, and economic dependence on men still characterize most women's lives. In the face of such negation, women embrace their role as Great Mother, nurturing children as well as men, and nurturing themselves with shared bitterness and love. Of course, both society and family prevent women from exercising and developing any real power. But "feminine" personality also stunts women's self-directed potential, their capacities for independent action, for achievement beyond primary relationships to children and men. Women are not only plagued by external restrictions, the force of ideology, custom, and law. They are also hindered by internal absences: self-confidence; a joy in and desire for creation, assertion, and mastery. Since society provides no support systems (e.g., child care) for women to be both nurturant and autonomous, they are directed, even before they know their own minds, into living one kind of life. The price of nurturance—the Great Mother—is autonomy; the price of autonomy—independent action, career—is nurturance.

For men, the bondage of masculinity means forever testing the limits of physical endurance, ego isolation, and emotional independence while leaching women's nurturance through the back door of masculine privilege, marriage, and sexual love. Despite the claims and deformations of a competitive society on men, they continue to control and abuse women not only because it is "in the nature of things" but also because such power over another human being compensates for life's brutality by providing one refuge where love and tenderness are possible on demand. Unlike women, men enjoy both nurturance and autonomy.

In relating to a man, a woman in love encounters all the forces of a patriarchal world. She must fit into a man's schedule, be available when he is, cater to his needs, and follow the social mores of her time and place. In most cultures, it is men who pursue, who determine first sexual approaches and choose daily schedules and residences when marriage takes place. Despite American society's characterization of love as primarily the domain of women, the rules, arenas, and rituals of love, especially sexual encounters, are shaped by men for their advantage. Women fit into a man's world by playing an assigned role. Until recently, women's only choices have been whether they play well, badly, or not at all. In each case, the price is high: nurturance of men and acceptance of their domination, or autonomy without men and acceptance of a life plagued by emotional loneliness. In both instances, nurturance of women *by men* is rare.

For psychological as well as cultural reasons, women are expected to give more tenderness, sensitivity, and support in a love relationship than men, while men are held responsible for economic support and physical protection. Whatever emotional, empathic support men do provide is often meager, grudgingly given, and inconsistent.

Because of psychological development, women tend to give into, and merge with, a loved one (which mother-daughter symbiosis has taught them), while men tend to keep women at an emotional distance (which the threat of castration has taught them). In loving, women and men bring to their involvements vastly different expectations and behaviors. Feminine personality is fundamentally a definition of self "in relationship." Other people, especially loved ones, become continuous with the self. Merging develops into attachment, and soon dependency is formed. Among women, and between women and children, such dependence is mutual. But between men and women, such dependence rarely occurs on the same emotional level and with the same emotional depth. Masculine personality entails a definition of self which is emotionally distant, with strong ego boundaries. In the public world, these traits are considered advantages. But in relationships, such characteristics prevent or disturb emotional intimacy, nurturance of others, even simple affection. Men's relational difficulty throws women back on themselves, on children, and on other women.

80

Woman's primary role as nurturer, provider of love, tenderness, and comfort for child and man, is a direct result of her exclusive mothering by a woman, just as man's role as possessor and economic provider is a direct result of the absent but dominant role of the father. Thus women mother men as well as children; they form and continue relationships with men as extensions of mothering, gratifying and protecting men while resenting and loving them in a painful cycle of oppression, fury, and guilt. Love begins as desire, but is quickly transformed into self-sacrifice. Both complicitous and duplicitous, the "feminine" woman often responds as a slave does, clinging to her oppression with misery in her heart, occasionally striking out in a spontaneous burst of rage, later returning to her lot with a fatalism that is more deadly than complicity. An entire subculture is likely to develop here, with women sharing bitter tales about their husbands or lovers, complaining about their inadequacies, their cruelties, their foolish attempts to "be men." This kind of "sisterhood" is formed from negativity, from a desperate need to be heard, recognized, consoled. Beyond temporary support, such community fails to challenge men's existing power and their lines of control over women's time, bodies, and minds. In using their energies to complain about men, women give up an opportunity to leave them, to form a community of women, and to pursue their own projects.

81

Within a patriarchal world, women's deep capacity for love is likely to mean a life of emotional pain, a yearning after idealized love, and frustration and bitterness in later life. For men, relational inability is likely to mean a peculiar kind of loneliness, a sense of never having quite fulfilled a woman or a glorying in power and manipulation, indeed superiority, at their capacity to call forth nurturance and love from women without reciprocating. This latter attitude has characterized the cultural norm of men's sexual approach to women, where woman's body is merely the ground upon which men have acted out their possessive or masturbatory desires.

Summary

The unequal conditions under which women and men come to intimacy and relationship are first set in our infancy, where the exclusive role of our mothers creates different relational needs in our psyches. Throughout the rest of childhood and adolescence, these needs are reinforced and increased by gender condi-

82

tioning, custom, and social interaction until "masculinity" and "femininity" are part of our deepest selves. As a result, relationships between men and women rarely occur with any degree of real equality, for such equality would have to exist in a world constantly provoking behaviors of dominance, "masculinity," and subordinance, "femininity."

By definition, design, and practice, love is experienced and expressed unequally by women and by men. Yet, because of our maturational processes, we remain tied to fundamental human needs for both nurturance and autonomy. Put another way, human beings, male and female alike, have needs for kinship and love as well as agency and individuality. But our historical, experiential reality has been that only men receive institutional, ideological, and actual gratification of their needs in a continuous, stable fashion. A man's world is *precisely* a man's world, because he is more free, more in control, more powerful than a woman. If she were as equally free, as equally powerful as man, the world would no longer be his province.

Indeed, women do not yet inhabit, although many have imagined, a world where both autonomy and nurturance are possible. The common condition of womanhood is a denial of autonomy within a life of sacrifice, and nurturance of others. Until men nurture women in the same way and with the same tenderness, and until women experience the same opportunities, psychological as well as institutional, to be creative and autonomous, equality—in love or anything else—will remain an ideal, a fantasy of the future. The choice for women now is to make their lives within a praxis of pain, limiting the expression of their own humanity as they cushion man's inhumanity to himself and others, or to begin refusing support to men in quite the same sacrificial way, while developing their own visions, their own communities, where nurturance and autonomy are everyday realities.

What these visions entail and how feminists imagine their fulfillment is the subject of the next part.

Notes

1. Nancy Chodorow, *The Reproduction of Mothering* (Berkeley: University of California Press, 1978), p. 10.

2. For a feminist criticism of both Chodorow and Dorothy Dinnerstein, see Pauline Bart, "Review of Chodorow's *The Repro-

duction of Mothering," in *Mothering: Essays in Feminist Theory*, ed. Joyce Trebilcot (Totowa, N.J.: Rowman and Allanheld, 1984), pp. 147–152. See also, in the same volume, Iris Young's more inclusive critique (which encompasses Jane Flax, Gayle Rubin, Nancy Hartsock, and Sandra Harding, as well as Chodorow and Dinnerstein), "Is Male Gender Identity the Cause of Male Dominance?" pp. 129–146.

3. Chodorow, *The Reproduction of Mothering*, pp. 164–170.

4. Ibid., p. 169.

5. Gayle Rubin, "The Traffic in Women," in *Toward an Anthropology of Women*, ed. Rayna Reiter (New York: Monthly Review Press, 1975), p. 192. Also see Young's critique, cited above in note 2.

6. See Dorothy Dinnerstein, *The Mermaid and the Minotaur* (New York: Harper and Row, 1976).

7. Ibid., p. 61.

8. Shere Hite, *The Hite Report* (New York: Macmillan, 1976).

9. Chodorow, *The Reproduction of Mothering*, p. 200.

10. Ibid., pp. 203–204.

Part Two · The Feminist Eros

Introduction

In synthesizing a critique of patriarchy from representative radical feminists, I have combined the historic with the psychoanalytic, the philosophical with the practical, the relational with the structural. This is both a reflection of feminist theory itself, which constantly seeks to unify and embody, and the reflection of my own personal impulse to understand and interpret the world as an interdependent whole.

While searching for a language to name sources of strength as well as confinement, to analyze oppression and envision liberation, these feminists have spoken in many tongues. Yet their work reverberates with two themes: love (nurturance, care, need, sensitivity, relationship) and power (freedom, expression, creativity, generation, transformation). These themes—twin manifestations of the "life force," Eros—are sometimes explicit, as in the erotic work of the "three Marias," but more often implicit, as in the political writings of Millett, Firestone, and others.[1] Always, these Western feminists write of oppression in their roles as wives, mothers, lovers and as subjugated persons, stunted and bereft. They also write of dreams of liberation—achievement, a society based on human need and relationship, creative expression that is not bartered with love or money. All these visions are threaded through with an overmastering consciousness of the realities of patriarchal power, of a being-in-bondage. But they also reveal a yearning for another, more humane condition, a being-in-freedom. Feminists speak of two kinds of power: one that is often hidden, sometimes brutal, always insidious, and another that is open, knowingly tender, and intelligently supportive. They also speak of two kinds of love: one that is twisted, manipulative, or too self-sacrificing, and another that is charitable, easily reciprocal, and above all caringly, wisely nurturant. This feminist envisioning is born from women's life experiences, the culture of their everyday lives where love and power exist among the loveless and the powerless.

If we return for a moment to the Nature/Culture—Self/ Other distinctions, we see how they help to elucidate women's restriction to, and by, relationships of loving. No matter how basic to human life and association, these relationships—with children, men, and other women—have been judged more natural than cultural, more intermediate than primary, and thus less significant, indeed inferior, to what men have considered important: culture, possession, objects, institutions. Despite their obvious value to individual and social health, indeed, their enabling of generational continuity, these relationships are used to deny women the power of self-creation and a share in a society and a politics which does not define power in possessive-aggressive terms. As explored by de Beauvoir, the Self-Other distinction becomes an archetype of patriarchal power. The Self under Western patriarchy is an objectifying, acquisitive ego visualizing and using the Other as extensions of the Self. Here, the Self is understood as male, the Other as female. Patriarchal power is, above all, a *hierarchical power*: of the Self over Others, of Culture over Nature, Public over Private, Men over Women.

Moving from the lens of existentialism to the metaphor of colonization, feminists have utilized another analogy to explain their relationship to men under patriarchy. The realities of the life of the colonized—bondage, servitude, inequality—are understood by women as a restriction to biological and emotional mothering, as economic and political subjugation to men, and as fear, internalized and culturally reinforced, of physical vulnerability to rape and other forms of violence by men. Here, colonization expresses a power relationship which is both possessive and abusive. Patriarchal love, then, is also possessive and abusive, relying on personal and political domination, economic bondage, and physical threat. Erotic passion becomes a vehicle for vengeance, savage possession, even outrage and murder, under conditions of patriarchal inequality. The male-female covenant "results in mutual, if often unconscious exploitation by way of the carnal embrace."[2] Patriarchy corrupts both colonizer and colonized.

Through these many languages—anthropology, existentialism, Marxism, poetry—feminists have spoken of the internal and external forces of patriarchy. To these analyses have been added those of history, mythology, psychoanalysis, and socialism. Thus Adrienne Rich writes of patriarchy as the "sexual understructure of social and political forms," *the basic units of Western civilization as we have known it.* Gayle Rubin defines each unit as part of a specific "sex-gender system" grounded in the exchange of women for purposes of control and use of their erotic/reproductive capacities. When aggregated into the "sexual understructure," these units are characterized by Rich in poetic terms: the "Kingdom of the Fathers" (culture, public domain, *power over*) and the "Sacred Calling of the Mothers" (nature, private realm, generative *power with*). Nancy Chodorow takes up psychoanalytic metaphors to explain the engendering of "masculine" and "feminine," locating the origins of Rubin's gendering process and Rich's "Kingdom of the Fathers" in the Oedipal experience in the patriarchal family which channels and surrounds the "Sacred Calling of the Mothers"—the pre-Oedipal experience of the mothering relation. She supports Rich's distinction between patriarchal love and power and what feminists envision as love and power. The former is possessive and threatening (the Oedipal father as paradigm), while the latter is transformative and nurturing (the pre-Oedipal mother as paradigm).

Meanwhile, socialist feminists such as Zillah Eisenstein and Heidi Hartmann have attempted to link the system of sexual dominance over women to different modes of production. Both argue, convincingly, that patriarchy operates independently of the economic base even while modified by it. Women's subordination to men appears to exist across historical periods and is not amenable to neat categorization according to economic modes. Other feminists approach the family within the contradictions of capitalism, pointing out how the historic characterization of women as erotic/reproductive vessels is transformed by pervasive capitalist values of commodification and consumption into monstrous objectification. Within the family, women's burdens as nurturers are increased because of increased demands to mediate alienation brought on by capitalism's crushing exploitation of everything human, loving, and creative. Psychological-emotional experience thus becomes both more important and more difficult under capitalism, increasing alienation just at the point when subjectivity becomes more available. This effect, coupled with the modern disjunction between family and economy, makes of the family a reluctant sanctuary for troubled, wounded individuals who seek again and again the comforts of sexual love and emotional sustenance from women. Because women are the historical (erotic/reproductive beings) and instinctual sources (pre-Oedipal mother, first love-object) of gratification, they are at the center of capitalist alienation—as grotesquely manipulated objects in an objectifying society, as redemptive lovers who promise a false because impossible transcendence, as primal mothers representing the last sacred value in an otherwise profane world.

But for Marcuse, Zaretsky, Rowbotham, and others, women's historical situation at the center of the contradiction between personal life (subjectivity) and capitalism does more than entrap women; it places them in a privileged, revolutionary position. That is, women's erotic/reproductive duties and capacities (childrearing, emotional mothering, domestic life) encourage the development of a particular relational subjectivity which enables critical consciousness. Moreover, according to Marcuse, this subjectivity hinders the reproduction of the logos of domination, that patriarchal form of reason which connects masculinity with hierarchical power. For him,

> the recovery of the sensuous roots of individual autonomy through the critical faculty of memory, in particular the memory of gratification, emerges as a decisive mediation between the psychological and political spheres of life. Women . . . have a privileged access to memory, not because of their biological character but because of their historical relationship to the sphere of social reproduction, that is, their particular forms of social practice.[3]

Because of Chodorow's painstaking work, we understand these "forms of social practice" to be the asymmetrical organization of parenting, particularly women's exclusive mothering, which establishes greater relational capacities in women, thereby allowing them greater access to the memory of instinctual gratification than men.

As long as women have near-exclusive caretaking responsibility, their female children will have greater relational capacities. And it is these capacities which are the loam, the necessary precondition for the particular critical consciousness I am examining. This is not to say that other forms of critical consciousness cannot arise in women, but that the feminist critical consciousness I call the feminist Eros arises from the relational capacities of women. Moreover, it is this critical consciousness which enables the "decisive mediation between the psychological and political spheres of life."

Carol Gilligan's work on the different moral voice of women is one example of this "decisive mediation." As Gilligan's study showed, women do not need to be mothers themselves for their relational sense of the world to guide their moral decisions. The women in her study mediated between their psychological and political worlds by way of their own moral parameters. These parameters grew from their sense of interconnectedness and relationships in the world and their obligation to maintain and encourage both these qualities. Thus, the women she studied chose to have abortions—that is, chose *not* to be mothers— *because* they had a relational sense of the world.

Gilligan's work can be seen as a confirmation of my larger argument, drawn from Marcuse, that women's relationship to the sphere of social reproduction gives rise to privileged access to the memory of instinctual gratification. This access, in turn, fosters a critical consciousness—critical, that is, in terms of the patriarchy, of a dominating, repressive civilization.[4]

Women's erotic/reproductive duties and capacities (their "forms of social practice") mean that they are closer, psychologically and emotionally, to the crucial relationships which form the grounding of society. Steeped in these diffuse, affective, intersubjective relationships primarily within the family but also within the larger society, women live much of their daily lives under nonhierarchical, nurturing conditions. These conditions both resist the commodification of time necessary for market labor while simultaneously accepting the demands of a commodified family: the socialization of children for alienated labor in the market. Because child care and housework cannot be organized into ordered activity, most women experience their days as fragmented by a ministration to others' needs and intimate concerns which constantly break concentration and routine. Women experience a kind of "timelessness" under domestic childrearing conditions. While this "timeless" quality infuses women's work with a sense of immediacy and uniqueness, it also exists within a world already organized around a set "working day."[5] This contradiction appears to collapse women's *work* into their *life*, forcing them to mediate a false division while also supporting it. Women's primary experiences and expressive interactions both within and outside the family are simultaneously experiences of *life* and *work: life* in the sense of basic human needs and desires; *work* in the sense of alienated labor—enforced drudgery, self-sacrifice, and abnegation. Women's *work* becomes the sacrifice of their *life* through an infusion of *life* into others. Closer to the emotional, the personal and the interpersonal, women are nevertheless characterized and restricted by the emotional and the personal, creating intol-

90

erable contradictions: women's unique human capacity for relationship becomes, under patriarchal conditions, an inescapable chain of bondage. Thus women's experience of "timelessness" opposes capitalist organization of time, allowing crucial access to the memory of gratification. But women's roles as socializers and nurturers subjugate them to the demands and deformations of capitalist society. The very quality which enables women to envision freedom is used to enslave them.

The result is that women occupy a pivotal position. For Marcuse and others, women's mothering tasks, and their relative separation from the *work* world, encourage a critical, even revolutionary, consciousness in them. They are less subjugated by the performance principle, closer to the sources of the pleasure principle.

Of course, it is possible that women's mediating position may not encourage a critical consciousness at all. That is, women's "naturalization" within the "naturalized" sphere of personal life may result in a numbing, deadening alienation of the kind described by Betty Friedan as the "problem with no name"— emotional emptiness and grief. Moreover, most women under capitalism participate full-time in the market economy, suffering less isolation within the family than Marcuse acknowledges. Thus women may be more subjugated to the performance principle than Marcuse allows, although less subjugated than men because of women's childrearing tasks. Further, women's conditions might just as predictably give rise to conservatism: an all-encompassing femininity which defends women's exclusive mothering, asymmetrical gender, and the patriarchal family; a sensitivity which fails to embrace the necessity for social change; a passivity of mind and behavior which results from atrophied capacities and a weak sense of self.

And yet the growing presence of feminist theory within the Women's Movement appears to fulfill Marcuse's prediction of a critical consciousness. Political scientist Joan Landes concurs in her own analysis of Marcuse's feminist dimension: "Feminism seems continuous with the fact that women have always been less completely subjugated to the performance principle, and with women's potential to develop a new form of non-aggressive or relational subjectivity."[6]

What better evidence of this critical function of relational subjectivity than its appearance at the core of feminist theory as consciousness-raising. In her discussion of the differences between Marxism and feminism, Catharine MacKinnon has argued, in essence, for the centrality of women's relational subjectivity to the feminist critique of patriarchy.

92

> The marxist criticism that feminism focuses upon feelings and attitudes is also based on something real: the centrality of consciousness raising. Consciousness raising is the major technique of analysis, structure of organization, method of practice, and theory of social change of the Women's Movement. In consciousness raising, often in groups, the impact of male dominance is concretely uncovered and analyzed through the collective speaking of women's experience, *from the perspective of that experience.*[7]

Beyond analysis, this women's perspective becomes feminist through collective action. The spur to action is a utopian feminist vision. In the words of Temma Kaplan, "Recognition of the existence of female consciousness necessitates reorientation of political theory: by placing human need above other social and political requirements and human life above property, profit, and even individual rights, female consciousness creates the vision of a society that has not yet appeared."[8]

The Feminist Eros

The nuance and texture of this vision must be culled from feminist writings of the last fifteen years. There are but few handbooks to guide a curious mind through the collective feminist odyssey. Those books that attempt such a comprehensive journey invariably leave out some significant contribution, if for no other reason than that the amount of feminist writing is too great for the compass of any one work.

My own attempt is no different. The canon of feminist theory is large and grows larger by the day. Thus, the feminist work I have chosen to explore is not intended to be either comprehensive or exhaustive. My choices—from Adrienne Rich, Jill Johnston, Mary Daly, Robin Morgan, Audre Lorde, Cherríe Moraga, and a few others—reflect the efforts of women who have made strong contributions and left deep influences and who can be said to represent a substantial part of the feminist vision. I offer one interpretation of this vision, which I have named the feminist Eros.[9]

In the work of these women, the feminist Eros encompasses the "life force," the unique human energy which springs from the desire for existence with meaning, for a consciousness informed by feeling, for experience that integrates the sensual and the rational, the spiritual and the political. In the feminist vision, Eros is both love *and* power.

Part of a dialectical interaction between patriarchy and feminism, these themes appear as a protest of and an alternative to the wounded Eros of the Kingdom of the Fathers. Against patriarchal values of polarization and separation, radical feminists assert the healing values of synthesis and integration. Robin Morgan expresses one characteristic of radical feminism when she speaks of an "urge to unify," submitting her own creation of "metaphysical feminism" as part of the rejection of "patriarchal dichotomizing of intellect and emotion."[10] For Morgan, feminism insists on connections, demands synthesis. Ambivalence, complexity, and the dialectic (both material and philosophical) are basic to feminist thinking. Contradictions are not forever opposed, by gender, for example, or on a more conceptual plane, by dualisms of Nature and Culture, Self and Other. Within the feminist imagination, contradictions are accepted and continually transformed. Morgan rejects hierarchic divisions and dominating either/or systems in favor of the "blend of passion and thought," "feeling and ratiocination," a kind of "passionate thinking" which reiterates and enlarges a primordial wisdom lost under patriarchy: "The life comes first. There is no spirit without the form."

As an alternative to the false separation of mind and body, Morgan speaks of uniting the internal and the external, the personal and the political. She means the conscious utilization of women's understanding of life, of physical and emotional life, in the journey toward a personal-political understanding of the world, the historical yet subjective world. The knowledge that women possess by virtue of their intimate relationship to the reproduction and nurturance of life should be the guiding principle in their understanding and critique of society and culture. No more should women reject their "relational subjectivity" as a measure of reality or a basis for valuation and judgment. On the contrary, they should cultivate its best aspects as a springboard to wisdom and alternative imaginings. Culture and politics, including the organization of sexuality, should reflect an intelligent unity of mind and body and the primary priority of life and life's continuity.

Morgan's "passionate thinking" has resonances in Adrienne Rich's call that we "think through the body," and in Audre

Lorde's suggestion that women learn to trust and act upon the "erotic . . . an assertion of the life force of women" which can infuse their lives with a creative energy. For Lorde, the erotic is the sensual bridge which connects the spiritual and the political; it is the "physical, emotional, and psychic expression of what is deepest and strongest and richest within each of us, being shared: the passions of love, in its deepest meanings."[11]

94

Under patriarchy, the repression of our erotic selves has led to a crippling, deadening life. My argument has been that this repression is anchored in the sexual understructure which has twisted both sexuality and love into monstrous forms of oppression. Women have suffered particularly because they are defined by an erotic potential which is misconstrued as purely sexual and is then used for sexual/reproductive purposes. But, feminists argue, the true pursuit of women's deepest erotic knowledge—the kind of knowledge, for example, that springs from the mothering relation—should become the taproot of women's lives. The erotic, once understood, can transform the merely sexual into an expansive life-force, into a commitment to life which is grounded in women's experiences. The feminist Eros thus unleashes a desire—for creative expression, especially in the areas of sexuality and work; for balance among needs, particularly those of autonomy and nurturance; for sharing and interdependence without bondage. This desire is inimical to the sexual understructure, to values of polarization and commodification, to the power of men over women, Self over Other.

Feminists have made of their desire a passionate link between mind and body. Their search has led them to a multi-layered, intimate knowledge of the physical and the instinctual, the basis of their return to love through a return to our most basic inner feelings, those acute understandings of what brings joy and meaning. The recognition of these feelings is the beginning of a new knowledge which empowers, which carries us out of alienation, the numbing of our feelings, into courageous living: "passionate thinking" and "passionate living."

The function of the erotic is thus transformative, challenging the commodification of human beings and their environment through a primary assertion of life values: feeling above sensation, meaning rather than reflex, human relationship as the basis of community, a community which nurtures and empowers its members. Such an empowering, many feminists argue, does indeed have the effects Freud found so fearful: it is knowingly antiauthoritarian because its measurement is women's experiential knowledge of life as a reciprocal, sharing interdependence rather than a dominating possessive bondage; it is consciously "timeless," literally reclaiming time by uncovering repression and allowing the thread of need and desire to assert the priority of human relationship over structure, ideology, and aggression; it is a mindful alternative to achievement as ceaseless conquest through a living which is sensuous, and attentive to the needs of life before the demands of a dominating civilization. In freeing time from the bondage of repression, the feminist Eros is critical, indeed dangerous to patriarchal civilization. But it is the kind of danger inherent in challenge, in risk, in attempting something immeasurably greater than what is threatened.

The feminist Eros is akin to Marcuse's "sensuous rationality," a transformative reason—no longer the logos of domination—which is sensuous to the degree to which it comprehends and organizes necessity in terms of protecting and enriching life and the life instincts.[12] This form of reason, unlike the aggressive rationality of patriarchy, evolves from an appreciation of the beauty and tenuousness of life. In this sense, it is really a wisdom about life which supersedes and opposes a purely technical, instrumental rationality propelled by an inner logic of conquest. In both the feminist Eros and Marcuse's rationality, a mindful knowledge of the body and its needs (a kind of logic of the senses) becomes the basis of a symbiotic relationship between the mind and the instincts. The sexual impulses are not blunted and sublimated for purposes of domination but are integrated into healthy, nonhierarchical forms of expression. There is an incorporation of the body into the spirit. Rather than "slime" or source of evil and temptation, the body becomes the ground, the lighting, guiding force upon which the daily living of collective life is enacted.

As Marcuse has argued and as feminists confirm, the capacity to imagine and embody a "sensuous rationality" depends on the material/psychological conditions of life. Women's *relational subjectivity* can give rise to such capacities, particularly through the care and protection of life, that is, through mothering.

The Role of Mothering in the Feminist Eros

The crucial importance of the relationship to the mother for understanding women's erotic/reproductive characterization and subjugation, their "relational capacities," and the feminist response cannot be overemphasized. The focus on the mother is complex, detailed, and pervaded by the deepest of emotional and psychological meanings. Thus Adrienne Rich analyzes how the mother, not the father, is the primal source of both love and power and how patriarchy has deformed this reality while restricting women to the mothering role. In explaining the nature of relational subjectivity, Rich argues that women understand, especially in their roles as mothers, how the beauty and simplicity of the mother-child bond is twisted and broken by the necessities of patriarchal culture. It is not only that sons go off to war, that daughters are traded to other, would-be fathers, and that the hierarchy of possession, aggression, and conquest continues to subvert feeling and love in a self-perpetuating "deadly" game. Even mothers who are relatively independent (*relatively*, because in a society where male privilege benefits *all* men, women who do not suffer the domination of a particular man in an intimate relationship are still subjugated to the larger system) must conform to the regulations of patriarchy.

> . . . every mother must deliver her children over within a few years of their birth to the patriarchal system of education, of law, of religion, of sexual codes; she is, in fact, *expected* to prepare them to enter that system without rebelliousness or "maladjustment" and to perpetuate it in their own adult lives. Patriarchy depends on the mother to act as a conservative influence, imprinting future adults with patriarchal values even in those early years when the mother-child relationship might seem most individual and private; it has also assured through ritual and tradition that the mother shall cease, at a certain point, to hold the child—in particular the son—in her orbit.[13]

Another feminist perspective on the mother involves an analysis of how the infant experiences enculturation, learns about its body and love and dependence on another, and grows to maturity forever imprinted with the memory of its first intimate relationship. We have explored Nancy Chodorow's psychoanalytic perspective on this process.

From a poetic view, Robin Morgan has written of mothering as the first relation in which we learn to fear and celebrate the body. When she writes that "there is no spirit without the form," she is asserting, in part, a mother's knowledge of the primacy of the body and its necessities. Life of the body (form) precedes life of the soul or mind (spirit). She argues that it is in caring for the body, as a mother does so carefully for her infant, that we come to understand and accept the body's failures and limits, its vulnerability to pain and death. Indeed, our unequal parenting relationship in which mothering is exclusively a female role, prevents all of us from taking full responsibility for our own mortality which, as Dorothy Dinnerstein argues, we conveniently blame on our mothers.

Thus our exclusive relationship to the mother is responsible for our failure to reconcile our fears of mortality, which are consequently displaced onto all women as representatives of mortal flesh. Our sense of utter dependence on the mother, Dinnerstein argues, forces us to both fear her and love her. The mother is experienced as the contradictory source of love and power, of desire and fear. In one of the most eloquent descriptions of the mothering relation, Dinnerstein expresses the texture of this utter dependence:

> It is in a woman's arm and bosom that the delicate-skinned infant—shocked at birth by sudden light, dry air, noises, drafts, separateness, jostling—originally nestles. In contact with her flesh it first feels the ecstasy of suckling, of release from the anguish of hunger and the terror of isolation. Her hands clean, soothe and pat its sensitive bottom. Her face is the first whose expression changes reciprocally with its own. Her voice introduces it to speech. . . . She comes when it feels anxious or bored and provides the sense of being cared for, the interesting things to look at, touch, smell, and hear, the chance to use growing powers of back-and-forth communication, without which human personality and intellect— and indeed the body itself—cannot develop.
>
> The child is, moreover, physically dependent on her for all these things far into a period in which it is mentally developed enough to be, in important ways, aware of this dependence. The human baby, because it is immobile longer and at the same time very much brighter, has a capacity for *feeling* powerless unlike that of any other baby animal: it feels the bind of wanting to do more than it can do. It must wait consciously for the will of another person to relieve its bodily discomfort—to provide it with the sensory experiences that it needs—to keep it company. . . .
>
> The child's bodily tie to the mother, then, is the vehicle through which the most fundamental feelings of a highly complex creature are formed and expressed. At her breast, it is not just a small furnace being stoked: it is a human being discovering its first great joy, handling its first major social

encounter, facing its first meeting with a separate creature enormously more powerful than itself, living out its first awareness of wanting something for which it must depend on someone else, someone imperfectly benevolent and imperfectly reliable because she is . . . also a human being. *This tie is the prototype of the tie to life. The pain in it, and the fear of being cut off from it, are prototypes of the pain of life and the fear of death.*[14]

Dinnerstein's poignant rendering reminds us of Morgan's truism: "The life comes first."

On another level, Dinnerstein's own truth speaks to the emotional meaning of the cultural link between maternity and mortality. This heritage, Dinnerstein and other feminists have argued, has meant a web of disgust and negation of the body which has been displaced onto women.[15] The way out of this hatred of the flesh, specifically the flesh of women, is for everyone, women *and* men, to accept responsibility for the body's mortality. Rather than repress our bodily needs, which later return as a dirty fascination or morbid rejection of the body itself in the persona of female-mother flesh, we should integrate and accept the body's pleasures as well as its pains. Such an integrated acceptance is only possible, Dinnerstein and other feminists argue, if men share in the intimate care of children, for sharing both the burden and the joy of nurturing a life which is doomed, eventually, to death, means an inevitable sharing of the responsibility for bringing a child (and therefore culture) to consciousness concerning its own mortality.

The feminist argument here is persuasive. When men begin to accept their own responsibility for rearing children, they will begin to accept the flesh in all its sacredness and profanity, beauty and revulsion, achievement and failure. The child, and the child within the adult, will then no longer have the excuse of blaming the first parent for enculturation, for the agonizing process of individuation and maturation, for learning that to be physically human is all that we have on this earth. Such shared responsibility would negate the necessity of scapegoating women as filthy goddesses and virgin mothers, and of lionizing men as disembodied spirits conquering history. The destructive patriarchal bondage of Self-Other, Masculine-Feminine modes of relating might be dissolved, later to be replaced by relationships of greater reciprocity and mutuality. Conceivably, both sexes could then share equally in the material *and* the spiritual, and the agonies and joys inherent in both. Possibly, the inescap-

98

able condition of our species (i.e., our individual mortality) would not be blamed on Eve or Pandora or other fearful symbols of femaleness. Perhaps then, feminists imagine, Western men and women might begin to discover the reality of the truly human, rather than the merely male, condition.

Out of their varied analyses of the mothering relation, these feminists have been led to imagine a realm of living which is profoundly anticapitalist and antipatriarchal. In this realm, the body and its instincts are freed from the surplus-repression of organized domination. Women's erotic-reproductive capacities become rich sources of meaning, no longer tragic forms of oppression. Rather than living under the fear of our erotic selves, which keeps us obedient and docile, crushing the voice of authority and knowledge within us, we would live in full appreciation of our powers. This feminist Eros—the joining of our disparate selves through integrating our life instincts—is both a response and a threat to the alienation and subjugation of patriarchy. Releasing erotic impulses and using them as a ground for living transforms the point of repression—the life instincts—into a force for liberation. Thus a wise, life-enriching utilization of the power of all manifestations of the life-instincts—infantile, maternal, adult—becomes the continuing link to gratification.

What these feminists emphasize, however, is that liberating the instincts, either through the achievement of a certain historical stage of economic development or through a "resurrection of the body," is simply not sufficient in the struggle against aggression, against the domination of Thanatos. From their privileged perspective of *relational subjectivity*, these women bring new light to the common observation that repressed sexual instincts give rise to aggression. Aggressive rationality, Marcuse has suggested, is the philosophical justification of cultural aggression; it is the metaphysical end point of patriarchy in an advanced form—capitalism. Because rationality has been severed from the needs of the body, Eros (the life instinct) is increasingly deformed: Thanatos (the death instinct) achieves ascendance by way of aggression and conquest. This is how surplus repression becomes *power over* the life force—by perverting sexual instincts through savage repression in the interests of domination. But, feminists add, women's sexuality more than men's is abused and objectified, truly at the mercy of patriarchy, of brutal men, insensitive institutions, a woman-hating civilization. It is not only that the instincts are repressed but that repression is rooted in very old social forms which concern the regulation of

sexuality and the rearing of children and which are intention-
ally maintained for the domination of men and the subordination of women. Thus the forces of change need to be focused on
the sexual understructure: women's exclusive care of children,
the gendering process, the institutions of heterosexuality and
marriage, and men's control over the material conditions and
ideological and symbolic characterizations of women's sexuality.
In the feminist Eros, the intelligent reorganization of our sex
and gender institutions begins with a revisioning of the form of
our earthly confinement—the body—and the source (and curse)
of our first love, the mother.

100

Notes

1. Maria Barreno, Maria Horta, Maria Da Costa, *The Three
Marias: New Portuguese Letters* (New York: Bantam, 1976); Kate
Millett, *Sexual Politics* (New York: Avon, 1970); Shulamith Fire-
stone, *The Dialectic of Sex* (New York: Bantam, 1972).

2. Barreno, Horta, and Da Costa, *The Three Marias,* p. xiii.

3. Joan B. Landes, "Marcuse's Feminist Dimension" (Paper
delivered at 1978 Annual Meeting of American Political Science
Association, New York, 1978).

4. See Carol Gilligan, *In a Different Voice: Psychological Theory and Women's Development* (Cambridge, Mass.: Harvard University Press, 1982). I am grateful to Kathy Ferguson for drawing my
attention to Gilligan's work.

5. Landes, "Marcuse's Feminist Dimension," pp. 16–17.

6. Ibid., p. 17.

7. Catharine A. MacKinnon, "Feminism, Marxism, Method,
and the State: An Agenda for Theory," in *Feminist Theory: A
Critique of Ideology,* ed. Nannerl Keohane, Michele Rosaldo,
and Barbara Gelpi (Chicago: University of Chicago Press, 1982),
pp. 6–7. Emphasis added.

8. Temma Kaplan, "Female Consciousness and Collective Action: The Case of Barcelona, 1910–1918," in *Feminist Theory: A
Critique of Ideology,* p. 56.

9. Two examples of attempts at comprehensive analysis include
Alison M. Jaggar, *Feminist Politics and Human Nature* (Totowa,
N.J.: Rowman and Allanheld, 1983); and Marilyn Frye, *The Politics of Reality* (Trumansburg, N.Y.: The Crossing Press, 1983).
Nancy Hartsock's *Money, Sex and Power: Toward a Feminist Historical Materialism* (New York: Longman, 1983) does an excellent
job of addressing feminist theories of power and powerlessness
within the context of other theories of power. For three critical per-

spectives on some of the feminists I am presenting here, see Ellen
Willis, *Beginning to See the Light: Pieces of a Decade* (New York:
Knopf, 1981), and two articles in Carole Vance, ed., *Pleasure and
Danger: Toward a Politics of Sexuality* (Boston: Routledge and
Kegan Paul, 1984) by Gayle Rubin and Alice Echols. Rubin's article
is entitled "Thinking Sex: Notes for a Radical Theory of Sexuality"
(pp. 267–319) and Echols's article is entitled "The Taming of the Id:
Feminist Sexual Politics" (pp. 50–72). Echols's article in particular
is a caustic attack on, as well as a flippant misrepresentation of,
what she calls "cultural feminists" such as Adrienne Rich, Mary
Daly, Robin Morgan, Susan Griffin, and others. She accuses them of
idealizing women's sexuality and their so-called "female consciousness" and of vilifying the socialist left. She further claims that
all "cultural feminists" argue women's superiority because of
their experience with nurturance, which then becomes to cultural
feminists, the basis of a "superior" women's culture. My own interpretation is that women's mothering gives rise to a "critical
consciousness" (in the Marcusean sense) which is the basis for far-
reaching feminist analyses of patriarchy. Unlike Echols, I do not see
all (or even many) "cultural feminists" as biological determinists or
as more interested, in Echols's words, in "nurturing an alternative
female consciousness" than in "effecting structural change." On
the contrary, it is the "critical consciousness" of these feminists
that has given the Women's Movement some of its most cogent critiques of men's power and women's powerlessness while also providing many visions of a better and more egalitarian society.

10. Robin Morgan, *Going Too Far: The Personal Chronicle of a
Feminist* (New York: Random House, 1977), pp. 290–310.

11. Audre Lorde, *Sister Outsider* (Trumansburg, N.Y.: The Crossing Press, 1984), pp. 55–56.

12. Herbert Marcuse, *Eros and Civilization* (Boston: Beacon,
1966), pp. 172–196. See also Nancy Hartsock's discussion of Eros,
which includes references to both Lorde and Marcuse, in *Money,
Sex and Power*, pp. 254–259.

13. Adrienne Rich, *Of Woman Born* (New York: Norton, 1976),
p. 61.

14. Dorothy Dinnerstein, *The Mermaid and the Minotaur* (New
York: Harper, 1976), pp. 33–34.

15. See, e.g., H. R. Hays, *The Dangerous Sex* (New York:
Putnam, 1964); Joseph Campbell, *Masks of God: Primitive Mythol-
ogy* (New York: Viking, 1972); Erich Neumann, *The Great Mother*
(Princeton: Princeton University Press, 1972); Ernest Becker, *The
Denial of Death* (New York: Random House, 1966), and *Life
Against Death* (New York: Random House, 1959); Andrea Dworkin,
Woman Hating (New York: E. P. Dutton, 1974), and *Pornography:
Men Possessing Women* (New York: Putnam, 1979).

Five · Love—The Return to the Mother

In their search for a new Eros, one that exists beyond the power politics of masculinity and femininity, many feminists have made a return to the original mother-infant bond. Here, the intimate, affectionate interdependency characteristic of the mothering relation is suggested as a primary value of adult relationship. For feminists in movement toward a new Eros, this "return to the mother" is both literal and symbolic. It is literal for those feminists who identify wholly with women: lesbian feminists. And it is less physical but nevertheless affectionate and nurturant for feminists who identify with women as part of a family of sisters: women in sisterhood. In both groups, the tender, symbiotic relationship between mother and infant is the conscious foundation upon which the identification between women is built.

For many lesbian feminists, physical love between women is but the logical culmination of a deeper, more spiritual, more emotional bonding. Because heterosexuality has been institutionalized through male privilege and dominance, especially sexual dominance, heterosexual love is seen as bondage, exploitation, a painful dialectic of powerlessness. By contrast, lesbian love is seen as a choice for freedom, for affection and bonding within a relationship between sisters, creating themselves rather than reflecting gender roles. The predatory power nexus of masculine-feminine interaction is absent, many lesbians argue, because the male is absent. And with him goes the penis-as-weapon; the aggressive, rapist encounter; the denial of female eroticism and gratification; and the pain of relational incongruity. The entire baggage of patriarchy is thrown out, leaving women free to weave ties of passion and compassion among themselves. Thus women's capacity to give and take satisfaction from another body like their own in a relationship of love rather than aggressive power is the basis of this lesbian feminist position.

In their particular "return to the mother," lesbians feel a sense of recovery or reclamation of "rights" to the mother: "rights" to a woman's body and its nourishment, which patriarchy has stolen and given to men. This idea of the "recovery of the mother" is consistent with Chodorow's psychoanalytic argument that all children, because of women's exclusive mothering, are first matrisexual, that is, the first love object being female, our desires are first focused on the mother. In phrasing their love as a "return to the mother," lesbian feminists are making a conscious effort to emphasize the primacy of the first love object and the fact that it is female. Lesbians suggest that, once accepted, this recognition should trigger a political understanding of the great injustice which has been done women, as mothers and daughters, through institutionalized heterosexuality and male dominance. Thus, lesbians argue against the classic Freudian view of lesbian love as regressive, that the nature and the reality of love between women is progressive, for some lesbians even revolutionary, because of its political implications: lesbian love contradicts the patriarchal imperative that men shall have exclusive access to female sexuality. Chodorow, Mitchell, Rubin, and others have analyzed how the father's (culture's) possession of the mother (all women) forces both male and female children to give up their first intimacy for later compensations. Because of the prescription of mandatory heterosexuality, it is the father (and all men) who will possess the mother (and all women), and women who will be possessed by men, *not by other women*. Lesbian feminists, angered by this "theft" of the first love object, frame their statement of "rights" accordingly. Hear Adrienne Rich in her poetic voice:

> The daughters never were
> true brides of the father
>
> The daughters were to begin with
> brides of the mother
>
> then brides of each other
> under a different law[1]

In psychoanalytic terms, the girl's turn to the father and the establishment of heterosexual orientation are clearly understood here as secondary to the girl's first love: the mother. Moreover, Rich asserts an intermediate stage between mother-love and the triumph of heterosexuality: the love between sisters ("brides of each other"). The "different law" refers to pre-patriarchal (pre-Oedipal) times when women's sexuality was not controlled by men and could be freely expressed within the bonds of mother love (maternal and infantile sexuality) and later as sister love (lesbian and nonlesbian).

The texture and quality of female bonding have been a central focus of feminist theorists. It is through convincing description of this bonding that lesbian feminists make their case against the "theft" of the first love object. By vividly recalling mother-love, and by evoking a reciprocal, nurturant love between sisters, lesbian feminists seek to explain their alternative to love within institutionalized heterosexuality.

As in so many other areas of feminist creativity, Adrienne Rich has been especially lucid and eloquent in describing this unique female bonding. In a poem dedicated to her real-life sister, Rich elaborates on the yearning for the mother, revealing how the law of patriarchy is interwoven with a mother's love, keeping women apart (daughters from their mothers) in order to service men (sons and fathers). Rich's capacity to trace the connections between the details of memory and the structure of society is masterful. Her poetic rendering of the world of women leaps between cultures and across time, giving us lyric insights into the political and sexual experiences characteristic of women's lives.

> Remind me how we loved our mother's body
> our mouths drawing the first
> thin sweetness from her nipples
>
> our faces dreaming hour on hour
> in the salt smell of her lap   Remind me
> how her touch melted childgrief
>
> how she floated great and tender in our dark
> or stood guard over us
> against our willing
>
> and how we thought she loved
> the strange male body first
> that took, that took, whose taking seemed a law
>
> and how she sent us weeping
> into that law
> how we remet her in our childbirth visions
>
> erect, enthroned, above

a spiral stair
and crawled and panted toward her
. . . .

And how beneath the veil
black gauze or white, the dragging
bangles, the amulets, we dreamed   And how beneath
the strange male bodies
we sank in terror or in resignation
and how we taught them tenderness—

the holding-back, the play,
the floating of a finger
the secrets of the nipple

And how we ate and drank
their leavings, how we served them
in silence, how we told

among ourselves our secrets, wept and laughed
passed bark and root and berry
from hand to hand, whispering each one's power

washing the bodies of the dead
making celebrations of doing laundry
piecing our lore in quilted galaxies

how we dwelt in two worlds
the daughters and the mothers
in the kingdom of the sons[2]

For Rich, the discovery of lesbian love came midway in life,
after the birth of three sons and the death by suicide of her husband. In expressing her feminist metamorphosis, she does not
flinch from a critical examination of her grief at this late discovery and of the deepest feelings which it has unearthed. Indeed, her creativity—poetry and nonfiction alike—has been
concentrated on a feminist renaming of these feelings. She
speaks, for example, of patriarchy's success in dividing women
from each other:

Birth stripped our birthright from us,
tore us from a woman, from women, from ourselves
so early on
and the whole chorus throbbing at our ears
like midges, told us nothing, nothing
of origins, nothing we needed
to know, nothing that could re-member us.[3]

Rich then continues, without shame, to speak the common
criticism of lesbian love, *unnatural*, while giving it a new name,

106

homesickness, reflective of the feminist consciousness of the family of women.

> Only: that it is unnatural,
> the homesickness for a woman, for ourselves,
> for that acute joy at the shadow her head and arms
> cast on a wall, her heavy or slender
> thighs on which we lay, flesh against flesh,
> eyes steady on the face of love; smell of her milk, her sweat,
> terror of her disappearance, all fused in this hunger
> for the element they have called most dangerous, to be
> lifted breathtaken on her breast, to rock within her . . .
> *This is what she was to me, and this*
> *is how I can love myself—*
> *as only a woman can love me.*[4]

This "homesickness" for the mother Rich describes as yearning for a love that is filled with care, with a mindful, wise attention to protecting and enriching life. It is, as Rich names it, an "active gentleness" characterized by a continual "bearing witness . . . against the predator, the parasite," a love (unlike patriarchal love of *power over* another) with "no mere will to mastery, only care for the many-lived, unending forms" of life.[5]

Even in her poetic rapture about the tender, nurturing love found in the mothering relation, Rich continues to distinguish mothering from the institution of motherhood. She is clear about the difference between the basic, life protecting qualities which are part of the mothering bond, and the self-sacrificing, all-encompassing role of motherhood which patriarchy constructs for women.

The kind of mother love for which Rich is "homesick" is the kind of love most female-raised adults yearn for: the first unquestioning, accepting, primal, enveloping love which we experienced with the mother and which, as both Chodorow and Dinnerstein have argued, continues to form the basis of our adult erotic drives. It is a love which understands the fragility and vulnerability of human need and which seeks, again and again, to cherish and nurture it. This kind of nurturance is also a kind of strength—the strength and courage of nonabusive, nonmanipulative love. Rich asks,

> What do we mean by the nurture of daughters? What is it we wish we had, or could have, as daughters; could give, as mothers? Deeply and primally we need trust and tenderness; surely this will always be true of every human being. . . . But this loving is not simply the old institutionalized, sacrificial

"mother love" which men have demanded: we want courageous mothering. The most notable fact that culture imprints on women is the sense of our limits. The most important thing one woman can do for another is to illuminate and expand her sense of actual possibilities.[6]

108 Unlike Rich, radical lesbian Jill Johnston has argued that the "different law" of sisterhood necessitates a sundering of the "kingdom of the sons" and its replacement by a lesbian community—what Johnston calls a "lesbian nation." Although she begins her argument with an attack on patriarchal rights of the father to the mother, she focuses on the nonlesbian feminist. Despite their activism, Johnston asserts, "straight" feminists continue to accept men's patriarchal rights to women, *because they continue to sleep with men.* Her line of reasoning is too simple. Because all culture is patriarchal, all heterosexual relationships exist within the sexual understructure and are therefore shaped by the myriad forces of male prerogative. Thus no interaction, however personal and private, can escape the pervasive power of the patriarchy. On an intimate level, then, no woman can sleep with a man and fail to be confronted, if not assaulted, by sexual politics. Johnston says of the feminist who continues to grapple with this situation that she

> is an incipient revolutionary. She is a woman in revolt against her prescribed and confined feminine role but she has not yet envisioned the solution to her dilemma for she persists in recognizing the brute sexual prerogative of the male while seeking reforms to alter her condition *within* the male defined structures *dictated* by that sexual prerogative. The rights of the father to the mother. She has forgotten her own rights to the mother as she once experienced the same erotic and nutritive dependency on the mother as did her son and brother. Her conditioning has been so complete that she has forgotten.[7]

Lesbians, by contrast, have retained the memory of blissful merging with the first love object and are therefore, Johnston reasons, in a privileged position to criticize the heterosexual institution—that is, the system of male access to, and control of female sexuality.

> The lesbian is the key figure in the social revolution to end the sexual caste system, or heterosexual institution, for she is the clearly disenfranchised of the four sexes. She has abdicated her inherited right, or rather command, to participate

in the male privilege by association, through bed and marriage and even friendship.[8]

Far from being "like men," Johnston argues, lesbians are nearest
to the reality of *original* woman because they live the primacy
of women as the first sex, the Great Mother of all living things.
Because love for the mother was prior to love for the father and   109
men, lesbian love is a simultaneous recapturing/reasserting of
that primary experience. Johnston continues: "The lesbian is
woman prime. The woman who maintains or regains her integ-
rity as a woman. By (re) uniting with her feminine principle.
The reunion of the mother and the daughter into the true sister
principle."[9]

Through an interpretation of the Demeter-Persephone myth,
Johnston elaborates on her radical lesbian version of the "return
to the mother." Her understanding of the recovery of the "integ-
rity" of woman begins with an open rejection of men, followed
by a celebration among women of their primary love. Both heterosexuality and celibacy are spurned.

> The psychological archetype of feminine reintegration ap-
> pears in the Demeter-Perspephone myth. The loss of the
> daughter to the father is the lamented transition from matri-
> archy to patriarchy in which the mother-daughter became
> estranged from herself in service to her captor and legislator.
> . . . The reunion of the mother and daughter constitutes
> the essence of the Eleusinian Mysteries of classical Greece.
> Persephone is the primordial virgin. Her return to her mother
> is the return to the mother of her primordial maidenhood,
> her intactness, her inviolate integrity as woman or total
> being.[10]

Note that Johnston's use of "virgin" is in its original meaning:
she who is unto herself; without men, masters, marriages.

Johnston suggested, in 1973, that women identify with other
women in reclaiming their "virgin" status, by which she meant
unmarried (unowned), not chaste. This reclamation was to be a
form of virgin birth, or "psychic parthenogenesis." This theme
of self-birth, or more accurately, birth from the sisterhood of
women, has been repeated by feminists again and again. For example, in writing of her feminist coming-to-consciousness as a
"woman giving birth to myself," Adrienne Rich has echoed the
need for "experienced psychic midwives" during the process of
feminist transformation.[11] This need has been met, in part, by
the development of women's groups, communes, bookstores,

gathering places, that is, by a practicing sisterhood. The lesbian suggestion of "parthenogenesis" is central to the feminist Eros: autonomy with support, individuality within a community of equals; the growth of self alongside the growth of others; women giving birth to themselves. In the conclusion to her book *Lesbian Nation*, Johnston states unequivocally: "The order of the day for all women is *psychic* parthenogenesis."[12]

Sisterhood as the medium for parthenogenesis also appears in Mary Daly's radical apotheosis, *Gyn/Ecology*, in the form of "Sparking" and "Spinning." "Sparking" is Daly's term for the kindling of the fire of female friendship, and "Spinning" is her name for the feminist journey of self-creation through intricate knowledge, then open rejection of patriarchy followed by a transformative commitment to women. Daly's terminology is only one indication of a stunningly original contribution to the feminist Eros. In the largest sense, she has attempted to construct a new symbolic for women, replete with its own unique analysis, feminist language, and metaphor. Indeed, Daly has given a name to the feminist Eros of generative love and power —Gyn/Ecology—which she defines, not surprisingly, as the "reclaiming of life-loving energy." This energy, according to Daly, is "biophilic," that is, in love with and protective of life itself. Specific to women, biophilic energy or *gynergy* must be reclaimed from patriarchy. The process of reclamation gives rise to sisterhood. But the voyage toward sisterhood is often a furious battle.

> This claiming of gynergy requires knowing/naming the fact that the State of Patriarchy is the State of War, in which periods of recuperation from and preparation for battle are euphemistically called "peace." Furies/Amazons must know the nature and conditions of this State in order to dis-cover and create radical female friendship. Given the fact that we are struggling to emerge from an estranged State, we must understand that the Female Self is the enemy under fire from the guns of patriarchy. We must struggle to dis-cover this Self as Friend to all that is truly female, igniting the Fire of Female Friendship.[13]

The trauma of the battle can be so intense and lengthy, Daly asserts, as to threaten the development of sisterhood itself. Women may be co-opted by what Daly calls "false inclusion" into the centers of patriarchal power as loved ones or "token equals," including categories of token feminists and/or lesbians. True sisterhood, however, is not sidetracked by the system's propitiating. Indeed, sisterhood is different from pre-feminist groupings precisely because women are conscious of their coming together *as feminists* with women's concerns in mind. These concerns begin with radical self-affirmation. Daly is very insistent here about distinguishing sisterhood from male comradeship/brotherhood where, she argues, individuals seek to lose their identity. In sisterhood, the individual woman gains her self through discovery and creation. Again, the argument is that the absence of men means a new freedom to explore one's female self outside gender roles, work roles, learned responses.

> Whereas discussions of relations between men and women eulogize the so-called complementarity of opposites, an Amazonian analysis of female friendship/love dis-covers the fact that the basis of woman-identified relationships is neither biological differences nor socially constructed opposite roles. As Jan Raymond has observed, rather than accepting a standardized "difference" (femininity), Lesbians/Spinsters find in our authentic likeness to each other the opportunity to exhibit and develop genuine differences. Rather than relying upon stereotypic role relationships, Amazon friends/lovers/ sisters cast our Selves into a creative variety of developing relationships with each other. Since there are no models, no roles . . . to fall back upon, we move together and apart in ever-varying patterns of relating.[14]

Thus sisterhood, according to Daly, enables the growth of Self, a parthenogenesis of women defined and identified beyond men. For Daly, as for Johnston, ultimate freedom for women is obtainable only through a radical lesbian journey—the end voyage of feminist sisterhood. Rich, by contrast, is less concerned with advocating lesbianism and more intent on illuminating the actual strengths of women and the paths they must pursue for survival under patriarchy. But she is clear about the value of her own choice, and the price women pay for participating in the heterosexual institution.

From another world—the world of a radical lesbian Chicana, the world of people of color in the underbelly of white America—comes another voice. Vastly different in expression and content from the works of Rich, Daly, and Johnston, Cherríe Moraga's poetry reveals a side of the mother-daughter bond, and of the liberating force of lesbian love, that is beautiful and evocative, yet deeply imprinted with pain.

In much of Moraga's poetry, the forced separation of mother and daughter by the "Kingdom of the Fathers" is filled with memories of a mother's violence—to herself, to her daughter, to the passionate potential of her life crushed by poverty and a repressive husband. In "La Dolce Culpa," for example, Moraga "returns to the mother" by asking agonizing questions. The refrain "What kind of lover have you made me, mother" begins each of the four parts of the poem.

In the first section, Moraga gives a stunning example of Rich's view that "The daughters were to begin with / brides of the mother."

> What kind of lover have you made me, mother
> who drew me into bed with you at six/sixteen
> oh, even at sixty you do still
> lifting up the blanket with one arm
> lining out the space for my body with the other
>
>> as if our bodies still
>> beat inside the same skin
>> as if you never noticed
>> when they cut me
>> out
>> from you.

The memory of early "mother love" is then brutalized by later years of fighting and separation between a sexually oppressed mother and her rebellious daughter.

> What kind of lover have you made me, mother
> who took belts to wipe this memory from me
>
>> the memory of your passion
>> dark & starving, spilling
>> out of rooms, driving
>> into my skin, cracking
>> & cussing in spanish
>>
>> the thick dark *f* sounds
>> the *c*'s splitting
>> the air like blows
>>
>> *you would get a rise out of me*
>> *you knew it in our blood*
>> *the vision, of my rebellion*

The memory, in turn, is followed by Moraga's painful recognition of her mother's sexual-emotional deprivation and how that deprivation, that oppression, divided the two women in the "Kingdom of the Fathers."

> What kind of lover have you made me, mother
> who put your passion on a plate for me

nearly digestible. Still trying to swallow
the fact that we lived most of our lives
with the death of a man
whose touch ran
across the surface of your skin
never landing nightly
where you begged it
to fall

> to hold your desire
> in the palm of his hand
> for you to rest there
> for you to continue.

And finally, Moraga evokes the bitter legacy of the patriarchy by asking:

What kind of lover have you made me, mother
so in love

with what is left
unrequited.

But if the "return to the mother" is filled with layers of hurt for Moraga, she uses her pain as a reservoir of strength. In a defiant poem called "What Is Left," Moraga says to her brutalized mother that love shall replace violence between them.

Mama
I use you
like the belt
pressed inside your grip
seething for contact

I take
what I know
from you and want
to whip this world
into shape
    the damage
has defined me
as the space you provide
for me in your bed

. . . .
I was not to raise an arm against you
But today
I promise you
I *will* fight back
Strip the belt from your hands

and take you

into
my arms.

Here, the images of physical and psychological beatings—
"belt," "whip," "damage"—are defeated by Moraga's triumphant
love for her mother.[15]

114

The lesbian version of the "return to the mother" focuses on
a repudiation of the sexual politics of institutionalized heterosexuality, especially the patriarchal separation of women from
each other. This rejection is argued through an assertion of the
lesbian alternative: women without men; women as sisters and
lovers. Part of this focus concerns the greater possibility for
emotional reciprocity within lesbian relationships. Here it is argued that a recapturing of intimacy and closeness is more likely
in lesbian love because women have deeper relational capacities
than men.

Another component of the lesbian "return to the mother"
concerns the similarity of bodies between lovers: many lesbians believe that physical gratification is more likely between
women because they are familiar with bodies like their own. In
this sense, lesbians agree with the physical argument of psychologists, Dinnerstein included, that women can more easily
provide a recapturing of infantile bliss because their bodies re-
semble that of the first love object.

But the recapturing of infantile bliss is essentially an
emotional/psychological experience rather than a physical approximation. Of course, physical gratification is an integral part
of lovemaking. However, feelings of merging and oneness depend not on whether the loved one is male or female but on
whether the loved one provides warmth, nurturance, and care.
The "return to the mother" is a return to love. Thus the
strength of the lesbian feminist argument rests more convincingly on the greater relational capacities of women and on the
increased potential for growth and freedom due to the absence
of sexual politics rather than on the argument of similar bodies.
The suggestion that female lovers are more likely than male
lovers to please a woman is persuasive only if argued from the
position that women are more loving and attentive—that is,
more relationally oriented—than men and are therefore more
likely to gratify their lovers than men. As Daly has pointed out,
the absence of prescribed role-playing allows a certain freedom
which, in the case of physical gratification, may serve to en-
hance lovemaking by allowing it to be more flexible, more ex-

ploratory, less bound by assumed responses and the fear of failure. If men would relinquish their patriarchal privilege while growing into expanded relational capacities, they could learn to gratify women physically as well as emotionally. Why so many men refuse to learn how to love and nurture is only partly accounted for by Chodorow's psychoanalytic argument but more tellingly explained by men's superior position in a patriarchal world. In order to nurture, men must abnegate power for love, share the mothering of infants, recognize women as their equals, and practice a mutual reciprocity. Few men, however, find equality preferable to a habitual, culturally sanctioned dominance.

115

In looking critically at this lesbian feminist argument, a few contradictions need to be considered. The "theft of the mother," while emotionally and psychologically descriptive, can never persuade the majority of women, even feminists, of the desirability of lesbian love. Realizing that women inhabit a man's world does not necessarily result in a repudiation of heterosexual relationship.

Partly because heterosexual preference is constructed at such an early developmental stage, and partly because genuine love and desire often exist even under unequal, exploitative conditions, women who may resent and resist the patriarchal system still choose to relate sexually and emotionally to men. Lesbian love must therefore grow out of real sexual and emotional needs rather than a learned political position. Put another way, love cannot spring from theory no matter how persuasive.

For this same reason, a "lesbian nation" is more useful as an incendiary threat in the feminist revolution than as a serious alternative. Since heterosexual relationship is the predominant sexual mode, it must be addressed as the major reality, not merely as one stop on women's continuing journey toward lesbianism. Women will continue to relate—emotionally, sexually and psychologically—to men. Lesbian theorists must accept this as a given. Of course, separatism as a necessary but temporary strategy should always be available, but it cannot be convincingly argued as a realistic alternative for the majority of women.

In many ways, the debate over separatism and the political versus sexual basis of lesbian love reveals how removed much of lesbian theory really is from most women's lives. It also reflects a larger problem within the Women's Movement regarding the conflict between "politically correct" behavior and sexual preferences. But more on this in Chapter 8. Suffice it to say at this point that such conflict threatens to divert feminist energy from more serious problems such as the death-nature of American culture, the grotesque exploitation of people of color, and the destruction of the living earth.

Finally, the "return to the mother" in these writings can also be seen as a basis for sisterhood, not only for physical love between women. The "different law" of sisterhood points to a world beyond patriarchy. Sisterhood speaks of symbiosis *and* individuality, nurturance *and* strength—indeed, all the qualities of growth, care, and transformation first experienced in the pre-patriarchal mothering relation. It is through sisterhood, lesbians argue, that freedom and love, desire and need, and integration and community for women can be achieved. The "return to the mother" speaks to the promise of a creative, nonpossessive kind of love: the love between sisters.

In their particular "return to the mother," these lesbian feminists have focused on a number of themes: (1) a rejection of institutionalized heterosexuality, and thus of love and caring under these conditions; (2) the assertion of a "different law" of sisterhood, which includes both the lesbian alternative and a community of women identified as feminists (radical self-affirmation, sisterhood); (3) an emphasis on a kind of relationship to the human and physical world which reflects the nurturant, generative qualities of the mother-infant bond and which implies a wholly different kind of civilization.

Nonlesbian, or heterosexual, feminists also work with these themes in their particular version of what I have called the "return to the mother." Two representative theorists whom we have already discussed, Dorothy Dinnerstein and Nancy Chodorow, have focused on mothering to explain the major force at work in women's lives. This focus includes how and why women mother, and how mothering contributes to asymmetrical parenting and gender, including the resulting hierarchy of public over private realms. Dinnerstein has argued that women's exclusive mothering allows both sexes to escape what should be mutual responsibilities: acceptance of individuation and mortality, and acceptance of nurturance and history-making. For Dinnerstein, women's mothering is the key to understanding nearly all our contemporary enigmas, especially the predominance of the Death instinct in Western civilization. For Chodorow, women's mothering explains much less much better: why the sexual division of labor depends on women's mothering and how the psychological capacities of mothering are reproduced generationally to support a larger cultural division between domestic and public spheres. For Chodorow, the impact of capitalism has been to increase women's motherhood role by separating domestic and public spheres, thereby narrowing the family to fundamentals of women's mothering, heterosexual marriage, and male dominance.

Both Dinnerstein and Chodorow explore the mothering relation in order to understand the enigma of women's subordination within the continuity of patriarchy. Both emphasize the repressive, deforming results of a sexual division of labor in which only women mother. The question of a different kind of love is secondary to the question of the relationship to the mother and its cultural effects. However, the work of both Dinnerstein and Chodorow explains the lesbian "return to the mother" as a more literal return to the original love object (through physical love between women). By underscoring the pre-Oedipal period and the continued symbiosis between mother and daughter, Chodorow's work in particular gives sound psychoanalytic reasons for the lesbian argument. Sisterhood as nonlesbian identification between women where love is experienced in a symbiotic, nonhierarchical way that recalls the mothering relation is also supported on the basis of Chodorow's work.

It is clear from the writing of Adrienne Rich, Cherríe Moraga, and other lesbian feminists that their idea of love is a philosophical, not merely psychological, concept. I have named this concept the feminist Eros. Nonlesbian feminists also share this concern with love as a form of the life-instinct. They too locate its origins in the mothering relation, while suggesting that love between men and women, not only between women, should begin with the simple but essential qualities first learned in the mother-infant bond.

Heterosexual women share the lesbian-feminist repudiation of institutionalized heterosexuality. But rather than emphasize the lesbian alternative, nonlesbian women speak of redefining heterosexual relationship by constructing more egalitarian forms of relating, parenting, and working. In the case of Dinnerstein and Chodorow, for example, the emphasis on the mother leads to the suggestion that men should share the mothering role which would have the dual effect of freeing women for other public tasks while allowing men to develop their own relational subjectivity through intimate child care. The effect on the child, male or female, would mean the reproduction of this relational subjectivity in both sexes. Thus a psychological exploration of women's mothering moves from a critical examination of asymmetrical parenting and gender to an argument for the restructuring of family and society.

On a more intimate, personal level another heterosexual feminist, Robin Morgan, has made a "return to the mother" via poetic rather than psychological channels. Like her lesbian sisters, she focuses on psychic rebirth and radical self-affirmation through the nurturing medium of sisterhood. She too reexamines the mothering relation from her position as radical feminist, renaming heterosexual love, sister love, and self-love by first renaming mother-love.

Conscious of the feminist focus on love, Morgan confronts the criticism that such a focus is typically feminine—meaning sentimental and not serious. On the contrary, she argues, women's historic obsession with love arises from their closeness to protecting and nourishing life. This love—the love which guards against the predator and the parasite—is, in Morgan's "metaphysical feminism," the basis of all life, the mortar which enables relationship, family, and civilization. It is not the self-destructive love of institutionalized motherhood and institutionalized heterosexuality but the love of nurturance, strength, and reciprocity which first appears in the mothering relation but which is subsequently romanticized and deformed under patriarchy. For Morgan, this kind of human love is the best approach to cosmic love. Thus Morgan reverses the Christian ethic which preaches that the love of God naturally leads to the love of "mankind." More often, such love leads to the hypocrisy and repression of organized religion which continues the split between spirit and body while reifying male dominance. To begin with cosmic love, Morgan argues, is wrong, literally non-human, since love as we first experience it comes not from the cosmos but from our mothers. It is everyday human love beset by limitation, confusion, and pain which is the origin of all later love. And the invention of this love rests with the mother.

In a beautiful long poem entitled "The Network of the Imaginary Mother," Morgan combines the twin themes of love and power characteristic of the feminist Eros. Temporarily leaving aside her emphasis on power, I will analyze her complex statement of the various kinds of love presented in the poem's five parts: The Mother, The Consort, The Sister, The Child, and The Self. The very divisions of the poem attest to the feminist themes of Parenting, Heterosexuality, Sisterhood, and Self-Affirmation.

In the initial poem on the Mother, Morgan grapples with an

118

acceptance of her own disease-ridden mother after years of estrangement and struggle between the two. During her mother's slow dying, Morgan comes to understand and accept the limits and failures of her mother, and the strange connection, seemingly inexplicable, which keeps Morgan tied to an old, bitter, stubborn woman. Triggered by the memory of her mother's smell when Morgan was a child, she writes:

> And this is the fragrance, almost forgotten,
> that warms the deepest dreams of us all—
> even the large male children who grow
> to fear, or conquer, or imitate its power;
> even the large female children who find ourselves
> rocking each other, or men, or babies—
> we, the living totems of that rhythmic breast
> that rocked us, and which we have become,
> yet long for still.[16]

Notice how Morgan has managed, in one short verse, to give a poetic rendering of the pre-Oedipal mother, of her formative influence on our adult lives, and of the yearning (Rich's "homesickness") for the mother's warmth and love.

Later, this understanding of the mother's presence in our preconscious and our unconscious, is expanded into an understanding and acceptance of the physical reality of our bodily life. Although I will explore in Chapter Six the feminist emphasis on the body, suffice it to say here that Morgan comes to her realization that the body precedes the spirit via an identification with her mother. It is through performing a mother's tasks—administering medicine and cleansing her mother's body—that Morgan comes to know "the life comes first. There is no spirit without the form."

In the second section, entitled "Consort," Morgan writes of her love for her husband of nearly fifteen years. Through their sea changes and divisions, their painful but often joyous discovery of themselves and each other, they learn about adult love by reliving the life-encouraging, life-protecting love first granted to them by the Mother. Thus, by way of another intimate relationship, Morgan is led back to that first love beneath and prior to all other loves. She says to her husband:

> Why have I called you "Mother" in my dreams?
>
> > And this is the question, almost unwhispered,
> > that wakens the riddled nights of us all—
> > the grown male children who dare not yet answer

what the grown female children yet dare not ask:
where is the reason for loving? who risked inventing it?[17]

Morgan answers, in her section called "The Child," that love begins in the mothering relation. Confirming Chodorow's analysis that a woman's mothering of her own child triggers a re-experiencing of the love and merging she herself knew as an infant, Morgan writes to her son:

Hush.
This is utterly simple.
Before you,
I did not know what it meant to love.
I did not know it was this:

Your outraged head
thudding stubborn against my pelvis,
turning itself aside again, again,
in your refusal to leave me.

The absolutism of your eyelids,
lilac-veined transparencies that swell
in rhythm to the rolling of your dream.

The authority of your mouth;
its gravity, tongue-frail,
drawing up the tide from my lunar nipples.

The visitation of that laugh
you abandon me to, unasked for, sudden,
miraculous as an underground spring
unlocking the Februaries of my life.

The summer-nap smell of your body,
the grace with which you stretch on wakening, animal,
the vulnerability of your baby penis, a rosehip
blooming shameless under my all unthreatened kiss.[18]

Here, maternal sexuality is mixed with infantile sexuality in a clear illustration of the basic bond which lesbians seek to re-create by loving other women, and heterosexual women seek to re-create by loving men. The point, as argued by psychologists, is here poetically made. We all seek to reexperience in our adult erotic lives that first mother love. A mother, through mothering, returns once again to that most ancient of pleasures.

In the section on the Sister, Morgan writes of love between sisters as the bequest from the mother, what she had earlier called the "matriheritage." Although the love spoken of in this section is different from the love of the Consort and Child sec-

120

tions, it is a difference of degree not kind, for the nurturance and life-enhancement which characterize Morgan's promises to protect both Child and Consort appear in the Sister section as a form of living already understood by feminists, that is, the feminist Eros. Thus Morgan writes to her sisters:

To nurture what we have delivered,
you must spin networks of survival
all of your own imagining.

121

This knowledge and advice, given in a bond of equality between sisters, Morgan expresses as a "token of welcome and farewell, a seal, a small gift, from one woman to another."[19]

In her final section on the Self, Morgan draws together all the forms of loving she has so elegantly described. In articulating a new symbolic which is purposely anti-Christian and antimale, Morgan fashions the Mother as sacrament, asserting both the primacy and beauty of the female.

As it was in the beginning,
 I say:
 Here is your sacrament—

 Take. Eat. This is my body,
 this real milk, thin, sweet, bluish,
 which I give for the life of the world.
 Like sap to spring it rises
 even before the first faint cry is heard,
 an honest nourishment
 alone able to sustain you.

 I say:
 Here is your eternal testament—

 This cup, this chalice, this primordial cauldron
 of real menstrual blood
 the color of clay warm with promise,
 rhythmic, cyclical, fit for lining the uterus
 and shed for many,
 for the remission of living.

 Here is your bread of life.
 Here is the blood by which you live in me.[20]

In a perfectly symmetrical conclusion, Morgan's radical self-affirmation follows on the celebration of the Mother.

Blessed be my brain
 that I may conceive of my own power.

Blessed be my breast
   that I may give sustenance to those I love.
Blessed be my womb
   that I may create what I choose to create.
Blessed be my knees
   that I may bend so as not to break.
Blessed be my feet
   that I may walk in the path of my highest will.[21]

Notice Morgan's deliberate contradiction of patriarchal ideology through her assertion of control over her own mind, body, and spirit. Finally, in a conscious alteration of a theme which appears throughout all sections of the poem as the phrase "I disown none of my transformations," Morgan says, "I affirm all of my transformations," ending with an assertion of the potential of female power:

There is nothing I have not been,
and I am come into my own power.
There is nothing I cannot be.[22]

Through poetry, Morgan has reiterated the major themes we examined in the lesbian "return to the mother." With the exception of the "rights to the mother" argument based on patriarchal theft of the first love object, Morgan explores all other points: our lifelong yearning—nearly thoroughly repressed—for the all-encompassing and all-accepting mother-love of our infancy; a feminist rejection of the bonds of institutionalized motherhood and heterosexuality through radical self-affirmation, which in Morgan's case entails the elevation of woman's flesh to divine status in a deliberate reversal of Christian emphasis on the Christ; the celebration of specifically female power in this divine feminist symbolic of the body and blood of woman (Daly's "gynergy" appears in Morgan's litany of her many powers: "brain, womb, knees, feet"); the celebration of mother-love itself as the prototype of a love which understands the vulnerability and beauty of human need and which seeks to nurture it; and finally, the assertion of sisterhood as one form of women's power and women's love.

Other feminists have returned to the mother in less masterful ways than Adrienne Rich, Cherríe Moraga, and Robin Morgan. Among these, Rachel Blau du Plessis, Carol Poston, and Jane Flax have made small but significant contributions to the feminist investigation of mothering and motherhood.

Du Plessis has framed her own preliminary thoughts about

motherhood as questions and criticisms of Rich's deeper study, *Of Woman Born*. She asks—against Rich's feminist definition of motherhood as "powerless responsibility" where the female takes personal blame for failures and suffers an individualized, guilt-ridden reality—if this description is not culture-bound. Since Rich is writing from within advanced industrial capitalism, du Plessis argues that her description of motherhood is only applicable under capitalist conditions where children are private possessions and where women are responsible for these possessions. Beyond this, du Plessis questions Rich's attack on generalized patriarchy, claiming that Rich blames all that is bad about motherhood on patriarchy while attributing all that is good to women. Both these problems, du Plessis suggests, arise because Rich "works and talks half-historically," that is, without due attention to the nuances of different historical epochs when motherhood may not have been a dominant feminine ideal.[23]

Although I believe that Rich documented her arguments better than du Plessis implies,[24] the latter's criticisms are important because they force feminists to examine motherhood in historical contexts. Rich does so, despite du Plessis's assertions to the contrary, but the point about the extent of patriarchy's culpability in producing what is bad about motherhood is well taken; indeed, it is the basis for Dinnerstein's and Chodorow's work. These feminists argue that women need to understand how our species' long infancy and our densely emotional/psychological memory of it are part of the inherent difficulty in parenting and enculturation. That institutionalized motherhood under patriarchy (e.g., the fact that only women mother) has made this difficulty monstrous also needs to be explained and understood. But the two realities *are* different, and du Plessis is correct in making the distinction.

Finally, du Plessis argues that Rich moves from a criticism of patriarchy's definition of motherhood (essentially an analysis of social organization) to an argument for women's repossession of their bodies as an answer to patriarchy (essentially an act of will). Du Plessis questions whether individual acts of will can have any lasting effects on changing social organizations, especially something as deeply rooted as motherhood. I think Rich shares du Plessis's concern, but has chosen to focus on the *experience* of motherhood and not merely the institution. This emphasis has been mistakenly understood by du Plessis as an assertion that a single act of will can alter an institution. Rich appears to be saying that women must control their bodies in every sense of the term in order for institutional changes to be lasting. And this control must begin with women's consciousness *about* their bodies grounded *in* their bodies. Rich does not argue, as du Plessis alleges, that some "unshatterable female spirit incarnate in the body" will rise up against patriarchy. Rich does believe that serious changes in patriarchy's institution of motherhood will not occur until women themselves reclaim their bodies and integrate this knowledge of their bodies into their daily lives. Acts of will are necessary (especially as part of the collective will) but not sufficient for institutional changes. These changes cannot occur, however, unless women move collectively to make them occur.

Beyond this, Rich seeks to integrate a newly celebrated vision of woman's body into her larger radical feminist vision of social change. But although her emphasis on the female body, particularly as she is a lesbian, is more specific and more closely tied to her arguments about the transformation of motherhood than du Plessis likes, I do not think Rich is an organicist in the sense that du Plessis means this. Du Plessis suggests that Rich appeals to biology, when in fact Rich appeals to woman's consciousness, too long repressed, about her body and its necessary relationship to her mind and her life (rather than its deformed relationship under patriarchal dualisms of Nature/Woman/Body vs. Culture/Man/Mind). Rich does not assert (as du Plessis says she does) some unifying, intuitive, biological sense which women possess as the answer to motherhood under patriarchal conditions. She does, however, argue that women should return to their bodies (as they make their return to the mother) in order to understand and transcend the false dualisms created and continued by patriarchy. Like Robin Morgan, Rich argues for women's celebration of their bodies as beautiful, powerful, and knowledgeable. Both Rich and Morgan ask that women listen to the rhythm of their whole natures: their minds and spirits in harmony with their physiology. Both are saying in their own way that "the life comes first; there is no spirit without the form."

Although it is not a major part of her analysis, love and its centrality to mothering are considered by du Plessis in her critical article on Rich. Here, du Plessis seems to say that mothering is not only difficult but contradictory, and that love for the child is the only answer during times when mothering is a "battleground." But behind her argument one senses that du

Plessis is less sure than Rich of the influence of patriarchy on the actual trauma of daily childraising. For du Plessis, so much of the burden of mothering is inherent in the process itself, no matter who shoulders the major childrearing responsibility. The "return to the mother" is a return to paradox, confusion, and painful love for du Plessis.

While du Plessis does not share Rich's celebration of the joys of the mother-bond, she does concur with Rich's argument about the pain of childrearing. The causes of this pain, however, are attributed more to the process itself than to patriarchy's institutionalization of motherhood. Why women, more than men, suffer this pain is ignored by du Plessis, and therein lies the major difference between the two women.

From another perspective, Carol Poston returns to the mother in an attempt to undertand the exact nature of the emotional link between maternity and mortality.[25] She is aware of Dinnerstein's explanation of one part of this link: our species' inherent fear of death is displaced onto the mother, who in giving birth also gives death; mothers are thus blamed, unjustly, for the mortality of human flesh; this blame accounts for women's oppression as well as a number of degrading cultural mythologies surrounding women. Poston is also acquainted with Rich's perspective that maternity under patriarchal conditions means the death of the mother's self through her sacrifice to the child, the husband, the nation.

But Poston is interested in the mother's own feelings of mortality at the moment of birth. She brings a new perspective to the ultimate contradiction that all mothers know: in giving life they also give death. Why is birth so closely associated with death? It is experienced by oneself. "Birth is a death experience because, like death, it is an act of essential solitude; no one else can die for us . . . no one else can give birth for us when labor is upon us."[26] It is experienced as the end of one part of the relationship between mother and child. After birth, they shall live as two beings, separate in their own flesh. "Yet another element of death at the time of birth is the death of the love relationship which has been developing for nine months between mother and child."[27] Finally, Poston, having experienced the infant deaths of two of her own children, says: "We mothers are all physical keepers of graves: and at the moment when potential motherhood becomes actual—the moment of birth—we are surely seeing that in giving birth, one commits another human being, if not one's self, to death."[28]

In elucidating a mother's view of the emotional link between maternity and mortality, Poston has taken back an essential part of the mothering experience, demystifying it. Dinnerstein's argument about our species' fears—of our separateness, of nature, and of the flesh—has been made specific to the birthing woman. Poston's return to the mother is a return to viewing the mother through her own eyes, her own words, her own feelings. It is a reclamation of one part of the mother's experience.

While du Plessis has questioned the meaning of motherhood in the broader context of childrearing itself, and Poston has asked about the connections between maternity and mortality, Jane Flax has explored the nature of the mother-bond from the dialectic of psychological needs for nurturance and autonomy. Flax's work parallels that of Nancy Chodorow, with many of the same conclusions. For example, Flax believes that the symbiotic bond between mother and infant is the primary relationship which influences all later relationships in life; that mothers relate differently to male children and female children, identifying more strongly with girl children, thus prolonging mother-daughter symbiosis; that this bond causes identity conflicts in daughters; that separation and individuation are more difficult for daughters than sons; that daughters undergo serious disillusionment and loss when they understand the relative power of male and female, masculine and feminine; and that this disillusionment is the result of patriarchy. Flax notes that the girl's lengthy individuation process results in a heightened capacity and need for nurturance (part of women's relational qualities), while also complicating her attempts at autonomy (which is valued more for the boy and which is therefore encouraged in him as it is not in the girl). The result, Flax argues, is that the girl is left in a painful bind. "She must choose between what feels like nurturance—the love of her mother, no matter how ambivalently expressed—and autonomy."[29]

This need for nurturance and autonomy is further twisted by socialization. Society teaches and rewards women for being nurturant, not for being autonomous. Flax argues that the hurt women suffer in their psychological development can be healed only when women are nurtured for being autonomous selves. As both Chodorow and Dinnerstein have argued, this kind of nurturance depends on a change in parenting to allow men the opportunity to learn to be nurturant while allowing women the opportunity to be autonomous.

Realizing that systemic changes to make parenting more symmetrical are a long way off, Flax suggests that women look to other women in their attempts to understand and resolve the dual need for nurturance and autonomy. Indeed, Flax believes that what women really seek, in their love relationships with men, is the love of the mother. (Once again, the primacy of the mother as first-loved and first-lost intimate object is central to the argument.) Flax goes on to say that the Women's Movement can offer an opportunity for women to resolve their conflicts with the mother (such as individuation, and love of the self) by providing both forums and one-to-one female relationships through which women can work out these conflicts. For her, only another woman's nurturance for one's autonomous self can give women what they unconsciously want. Given that women's nurturance by men is not forthcoming, and given that women have not resolved their desire or their fear of the mother, sisterhood offers both a practical and a psychological solution to the need for nurturance *and* autonomy.

Flax's work, like that of Rich, Morgan, and others, points to the rich potential of feminism. Again, a serious exploration of mothering has led to a new understanding of the interplay between structure and feeling, institution and experience. This understanding has enabled the formulation of new visions: sisterhood as one kind of practical answer to women's real needs. The love that daughters give up in infancy (mother-love) is refashioned as the love between sisters. In light of patriarchy's law that only men will inherit the love of women, Flax's assertion of sisterhood as a form of loving is a serious threat to patriarchy. Like the lesbian reclamation of "rights" to the mother, Flax's sisterhood promises women the opportunity (1) to heal deep psychological wounds (the loss of the mother, and female subjugation to the father/husband); (2) to achieve psychological wholeness (through gaining both nurturance and autonomy from women); and (3) to alter their conditions through a practicing solidarity (the Women's Movement).

In both lesbian and heterosexual feminist theory, the search for the sources of women's oppression has resulted in a "return to the mother." Part of this return has been an exploration of the mother-infant bond from the perspective of psychosexual development, gender identification, and sexual sociology (Dinnerstein, Chodorow, Flax). Another part has been a celebration of women, individually and collectively, and their prepatriarchal (pre-Oedipal) past. Investigations of mother-love become the basis for a protective, generous approach to life itself—what I have called the feminist Eros (Morgan, Rich, Moraga, Johnston, Daly).

My argument has been that the "return to the mother" has led to a feminist refashioning of love as the enrichment of the life instincts. This love is not romantic or typically feminine. It is, rather, a response and alternative to patriarchal love as possessive, abusive, and conquering. Love that is care, active gentleness, reciprocity, and nurturance is the kind of love which these radical feminists have distilled from the mother-infant bond and which they celebrate in opposition to patriarchy.

128

Notes

1. Adrienne Rich, *The Dream of a Common Language: Poems 1974–1977* (New York: Norton, 1978), p. 52.

2. Ibid., pp. 48–49.

3. Ibid., p. 75.

4. Ibid., pp. 75–76.

5. Ibid., p. 77.

6. Adrienne Rich, *Of Woman Born* (New York: Norton, 1976), p. 246.

7. Jill Johnston, *Lesbian Nation: The Feminist Solution* (New York: Simon and Schuster, 1973), p. 183.

8. Ibid.

9. Ibid., p. 185.

10. Ibid., p. 254.

11. Rich, *Of Woman Born*, pp. 184–185.

12. Johnston, *Lesbian Nation*, p. 258.

13. Mary Daly, *Gyn/Ecology: The Metaethics of Radical Feminism* (Boston: Beacon, 1978), p. 355.

14. Ibid., p. 382.

15. Both poems appear in *Pleasure and Danger*, ed. Carole Vance (Boston: Routledge and Kegan Paul, 1984), pp. 417–419.

16. Robin Morgan, *Lady of the Beasts* (New York: Random House, 1976), p. 64.

17. Ibid., p. 71.

18. Ibid., pp. 78–79.

19. Ibid., pp. 76–77.

20. Ibid., p. 86–87.

21. Ibid., p. 87–88.

22. Ibid., p. 88.

23. Rachel Blau de Plessis, "Washing Blood: Introduction," *Feminist Studies* 4, no. 2 (June 1978): 1–12.

24. Rich, *Of Woman Born*, pp. 128–185.

25. Carol Poston, "Childbirth in Literature," *Feminist Studies* 4, no. 2 (June 1978): 18–31.

26. Ibid., p. 29.

27. Ibid.

28. Ibid., p. 30.

29. Jane Flax, "The Conflict Between Nurturance and Autonomy in Mother-Daughter Relationships and Within Feminism," *Feminist Studies* 4, no. 2 (June 1978): 171–189.

Six · Love—The Return to the Body

The "return to the mother" has meant a simultaneous "return to the body" where feminists have learned that a mother's love —the love of life—entails a love and acceptance of the body. In this sense, the "return to the mother" is a return to synthesis because mother-love does not separate body from mind, spirit from form. From this perspective, the pre-Oedipal stage can be seen as the time when love is learned through intimate care of the body.

The "return to the body" is also a vehicle through which women come to accept their own bodies as beautiful and powerful sources of pleasure and creation. In the face of patriarchal hatred and fear of the body of woman, feminists have consciously celebrated both the erotic and the reproductive capacities of their bodies. Beyond the acceptance of their own sexuality, feminists have argued that women need to understand how their bodies work and how this body knowledge enables women to begin to think differently and positively about their bodies. As in the reclamation of the mother and her experiences, the feminist "return to the body" is also a reclamation of woman's body and its capacities from the ideological and institutional deformations of patriarchy.

Feminists have concentrated on the female body in an attempt to join spirit with form, to transcend the patriarchal dualism which characterizes the female as dank, dark sensuality while simultaneously exalting her as unconscious, virgin purity. In a larger view, the "return to the body" has also meant a celebration and acceptance of the human body, not only the female body. Thus Robin Morgan and Dorothy Dinnerstein speak of accepting the flesh and its limitations as part of their particular return to the body. And Adrienne Rich speaks of combining the wisdom of the body with the wisdom of the mind; this is the meaning behind her desire to "think through the body." The body as source of knowledge and pleasure, the body as source of pain and death, the body as home of the mind, and the female body as home of the child are all visions and versions of the feminist consciousness in the "return to the body." This emphasis, in Marcuse's terms, moves toward the liberation of the life impulses, toward the breaking of the bonds of surplus repression. By returning to the source of their oppression, feminists work toward their liberation.

We saw Adrienne Rich make her return to the mother through a reexamination of mothering and the institution of motherhood. For Rich, the "return to the mother" triggers a "return to the body" which begins, as with Morgan, at the conscious recall of her mother's smell, a tactile emphasis characteristic of the feminist journey. Rich says to her real-life sister in the same poem examined previously:

> Remind me how we loved our mother's body
> our mouths drawing the first
> thin sweetness from her nipples
>
> our faces dreaming hour on hour
> in the salt smell of her lap. . . .[1]

Later, this memory of the mother, of her comforting body, develops into a yearning for mother-love, what Rich has termed "homesickness." This "homesickness" becomes, for Rich, a yearning for the body of woman, for the nurturance and care which, she believes, only women can provide.

Because she is a consciously political lesbian, Rich frames her love of woman's body as both an act *against* patriarchy and as an act *for* the liberation of women. Thus Rich states her determination "to heal—insofar as an individual woman can, and as much as possible with other women—the separation between mind and body."[2] Part of this healing requires not only that women control their bodies but that they "touch the unity and resonance of our physicality, our bond with the natural order, the corporeal ground of our intelligence."[3]

For Rich, women's physicality is a resource rather than a destiny. This resource needs to be explored, incorporated into women's conscious lives, and made the grounding of woman's being. The "power inherent in female biology" needs to be defined and reclaimed by women. Part of this definition has been attempted by Rich herself.

> From brain to clitoris through vagina to uterus, from tongue to nipples to clitoris, from fingertips to clitoris to brain, from

nipples to brain and into the uterus, we are strung with invisible messages of an urgency and restlessness which indeed cannot be appeased, and of a cognitive potentiality that we are only beginning to guess at. We are neither "inner" nor "outer" constructed; our skin is alive with signals; our lives and our deaths are inseparable from the release or blockage of our thinking bodies.[4]

This recovery of the female body has a purpose: the "possibility of converting our physicality into both knowledge and power."[5] Such a conversion, Rich hopes, will enable women to do what patriarchy has prevented them from doing: close the wound of separation between bodily needs (including the enormous potential inherent in female sexuality) and active thinking; heal the hurt of flesh-loathing by men and women both; and recover a sense of female strength which moves confidently to protect and enrich life. It is in this sense that Rich says, "I am really asking whether women cannot begin, at last, to think through the body."[6]

Part of Rich's exploration of her own physicality has entailed an exquisite exploration and celebration of intimate sexual love between women. Rich has purposely traced this love back to the mother, asserting the primacy of the mother against the father and other males. In an ironic twist on Freudian interpretations of lesbian love, Rich claims the return to the mother as progressive rather than regressive because mother-love (and its manifestation as lesbian love) is nurturant, nonabusive, and protective of life. For feminists, mother-love and lesbian love are expressions of Eros, the life instincts, asserting themselves against patriarchal love represented by aggressive power, civilization as the logos of domination, and by Thanatos, the death instinct.

Rich's celebration of the female body has several purposes. First, and most important, is the open, public, and positive description of parts of the female body which patriarchy has deemed shameful, secret, or filthy. This public description not only brings foward what has been considered taboo but does so in a fashion and for a purpose which is also forbidden: as a statement of love for another woman. By challenging patriarchal authority in this manner, Rich has contributed to the reality of a new feminist symbolic, reclaiming the female body by describing it with love and passion. She has also given other women the opportunity to see themselves as beautiful and powerful through the knowing eyes of a woman rather than through the patriarchal eyes of men, where the female body is so often seen as disgusting and/or threatening.

Second, Rich has challenged the patriarchal imperative of heterosexuality. By evoking a tremendous eroticism between women, Rich offers an alternative to heterosexual love while contradicting the patriarchal law that men shall have exclusive access to female sexuality.

Finally, Rich's treatment of lesbian love as *preferable* to heterosexual love under existing patriarchal conditions is a bold, even dangerous posture. Regardless of its persuasive power, such an approach is a brilliant reversal of historical and contemporary treatments of lesbianism as the result of unsatisfactory heterosexual encounters. Rich, with other lesbian feminists, is saying quite clearly: I prefer women because I love their bodies; heterosexuality, no matter how pleasurable, cannot compare with lesbian love for me.

For many, Rich's position is shocking and exclusive. Yet, Rich has been consistent in her attack on institutionalized heterosexuality rather than heterosexual preference. She has also not asserted, as has Jill Johnston, for example, that women who are heterosexual are inferior to women who are lesbians. What Rich has done, however, is to give eloquence to the wonders of women loving other women. By so doing, she has contributed to women's reclamation of the female body, of female sexuality, and of the entire naming of the female anatomy. For example, note in the following poem how the vulva, vagina, and clitoris are described as a "rose-wet cave," a far cry from the "gash," "hole," and "wound" of patriarchal descriptions.[7]

> Whatever happens with us, your body
> will haunt mine—tender, delicate
> your lovemaking, like the half-curled frond
> of the fiddlehead fern in forests
> just washed by sun. Your traveled, generous thighs
> between which my whole face has come and come—
> the innocence and wisdom of the place my tongue has
>   found there—
> the live, insatiate dance of your nipples in my mouth—
> your touch on me, firm, protective, searching
> me out, your strong tongue and slender fingers
> reaching where I had been waiting years for you
> in my rose-wet cave—whatever happens, this is.[8]

Part of the feminist "return to the body" has been the assertion that women's sexuality can be fully explored and appreciated only through relationships with women. As mentioned in the previous section on the "return to the mother," this argument for lesbianism proceeds from a biological point: because women's bodies are similar—both to each other, and to the original love object, the mother—women are more likely than men to satisfy other women. In this particular statement of lesbian love, it is important to remember that a *physical* case is being argued, not merely an emotional or relational case. Jill Johnston is an excellent representative of this position. She is well aware of Freudian psychology and its permutations, and also of the subtle causal links between physical gratification and emotional bonding. She says of the possibilities of lesbian love:

> Not only is the psychic-emotional potential for satisfaction with another woman far greater than that with a man, insomuch as every woman like every man was originally most profoundly attached to herself as her mother, but there is more likelihood of sexual fulfillment with another woman as well since all organisms best understand the basic equipment of another organism which most closely resembles themselves.[9]

Since women can best achieve relational and sexual fulfillment with other women, they should give up men (withdraw from them sexually) and begin asserting their sexuality with other women. "The first order of business for a woman is the redefinition of herself through assertion of her sexuality in relation to herself or her own equal, in other words, independently of the man."[10]

Johnston arrived at this theoretical position by other avenues as well. Besides the argument that woman's body provides a more fulfilling "return to the mother," Johnston noted how the much publicized failure of men to satisfy women (not merely an American phenomenon, considering the work of Portugal's "three Marias") forced feminists to look critically at heterosexual relationships. For example, Johnston argued, feminism added a new context to the problem of female frigidity. Perhaps women failed to achieve orgasm (not to mention love and affection) with men because men were bad lovers.

> I really think the feminists basically were making a common complaint in the new terminological context of feminism. That the man was no good in bed. That he was insensitive to the essential clitoris. That he just didn't know how to do it. And as an added fillip the new challenge that a woman or feminist anyway would henceforth refuse to accept responsibility for a frigidity that wasn't her own fault.[11]

136

Rather than wait for men to become sensitive lovers (which they would have no incentive to become, given their own satisfaction in heterosexual relationships and their belief that it is women's responsibility not men's to nurture and please), women should come to understand their own sexuality with other women. In practical terms, this meant appreciating the sensitivity of the clitoris and the vagina and the fact that penile penetration was not necessary for female orgasm.

By arguing this point, Johnston reversed the cultural mythology which pictured women as dependent on an erect penis for sexual gratification. She argued, with plenty of supporting evidence from sex researchers Masters and Johnson, that women could achieve sexual satisfaction without men. If this were the case, then heterosexuality was problematic for women on at least three fronts: relationally, sexually, and politically. In her version of the "return to the mother," Johnston had made an argument for lesbianism from the perspective of power politics. Rejection of men meant rejection of male privilege and dominance, and an embrace of sisterhood for self-growth and self-determination (parthenogenesis). In her "return to the body," Johnston attacked male supremacy by arguing that men were incompetent in both love and sex: they could not *feel* love or *make* love. Thus heterosexual relationships, according to Johnston's withering analysis, had nothing but oppression to recommend them. Given this condition, Johnston posed the alternative for feminists quite clearly. "If you're not part of the solution, you're part of the problem. A personal solution or exceptional adjustment to a political problem is a collusion with the enemy. The solution is getting it together with women. Or separatism."[12] Johnston was one of the early supporters of the radical lesbian position which claimed, "Feminism is the theory, lesbianism is the practice."

Johnston's arguments were prophetic harbingers of later developments in feminist theory, prefiguring the emphasis on the mother and the body, and the increasing tension between theory and praxis. After Johnston, lesbian feminists came more and more to a public celebration of emotional and physical love between women. They also engaged the entire question of separatism in a face-to-face confrontation with heterosexual feminists. Although it is difficult to assess the influence of the lesbian feminist celebration of the female body on general social attitudes, I think it fair to say that the lesbian contribution to women's struggle to reclaim their sexuality has been substantial. Because lesbians have focused so intently on naming parts of the female body in terms of beauty and passion, they have encouraged women to think positively about their bodies, their sexual needs, and the whole area of heterosexual relationships. With increased public discussion of orgasm, of sexual preference, and of the human need for sexual expression and gratification has come a change in attitudes and behavior. By their public posture and theoretical arguments, as well as by their private lives of loving and supporting women, lesbians have helped women to challenge patriarchal thinking and control over women's bodies. Beyond this, lesbians have encouraged a liberation of the sexual instincts from the surplus repression of mandatory heterosexuality. For them, the "return to the body" is more literal and more central to feminism than it is for many heterosexual feminists.

From a totally different perspective, Cherríe Moraga has argued a "return to the body" as an acceptance of lesbian desire in the face of strong cultural disapproval and personal denial. Unlike Rich and Johnston, Moraga's world is steeped in the poverty and racism of Third World Americans. The struggle out of this world is a multilayered struggle against heterosexism, white cultural dominance, and the internalized values that serve to maintain both. For Moraga, the process of discovery, reclamation, and assertion of her lesbian sexuality is enormously painful, even while it is liberating. Indeed, the title of her book of poems and essays, *Loving in the War Years*, is an indication of just how much struggle her lesbian feminist evolution has demanded of her. Although she shares the yearning for mother-love that Rich describes, Moraga's "homesickness" is edged with sorrow and a profound sense of the cost of her choice. When she celebrates the body of woman loved by other women, it is mixed with the hurt of lifelong wounds from poverty, insecurity, and cultural and female oppression. For Moraga, mother-love and lesbian love are inseparable, but their joining is also a reminder of pain and deprivation, hardness and softness.

> For you, mama, I have unclothed myself before a woman
> have laid wide the space between my thighs
> straining open the strings held there
> taut and ready to fight.
>
> Stretching my legs and imagination so open
> to feel my whole body cradled
> by the movement of her mouth, the mouth

of her thighs rising and falling, her arms
her kiss, all the parts of her open
like lips moving, talking me into loving.
I remember this common skin, mama
oiled by work and worry.
Hers is a used body like yours
one that carries the same scent
of silence   I call it home.[13]

138

Moraga's "return to the body," as her "return to the mother," is
an agonizing journey home.

As different from Moraga as she is from Rich and Johnston,
heterosexual feminist Robin Morgan has emphasized an acceptance of the human body itself, a celebration of the erotic and
creative potential of the female body and a recovery of women's
control over their own bodies, particularly sexuality and reproduction. Like Rich and Johnston, Morgan's "return to the body"
flows from a search for the essential life instincts. The creation
of a feminist symbolic which defines and asserts the primacy of
Eros over Thanatos is what these feminists are about. For them,
the body is the home of love, the place where love is born and
where it dies.

Illustrating the feminist principles of integration and synthesis, the "return to the mother" has been a simultaneous
"return to the body." Thus Morgan writes to her child in the
"Network of the Imaginary Mother":

This you have taught me—what it is to love.
Your unmodern wisdom thudding against my pelvis,
refusing to leave me.
How can I not celebrate
this body,
your first home?[14]

The child teaches love—love of the body, love of another, love of
life itself. Morgan writes:

This blood is my own, of my own making.
Flesh of my flesh. These breasts were all you knew.
Before this, I did not understand
the luxury of skin, its velvet imperative.
You have taught me
the most ancient of pleasures.[15]

We saw earlier what Morgan meant by the "luxury of skin": her
infant son and his nursing mouth; her responsive "lunar nip-

ples"; his "baby penis . . . blooming shameless" under Morgan's "unthreatened kiss"; the contractions of his birth, and the actual push against her pelvis. Here, the "velvet imperative" of the body's pleasures are learned during the long symbiosis of the mother-infant bond.

But the body also brings pain, deformity, and shame as well as gratification and joy. Morgan accepts this contradiction, naming and renaming the *despicable* in her recovery of the body and her acceptance of mortality. For her, the naming of the body's decay is necessary for its acceptance. In caring for her dying mother, Morgan comes to terms with her revulsion of diseased flesh, finally acknowledging the body's awful vulnerability. In light of Dinnerstein's analysis of the cultural link between maternity and mortality, it is significant that Morgan comes to her realization while cleansing her mother's genitals and helping her to urinate. Morgan is quite aware, as the following excerpt reveals, of the symbolic and actual importance of the female genitals for sexuality and fertility. By joining these values to the horrible realities of dying, Morgan has confronted the paradox of birth and death. In so doing, she repudiates patriarchal repression of the body's vulnerabilities and their displacement onto women.

> Vile. This is vile. This is the Mystery
> from which my inmost flesh-revulsion springs.
> This loathing, now, to kneel between these massive thighs
> squatting in pain; to bear this bedpan like a chalice
> for the dregs of her life's untold hagiography;
> to lie such set responses of encouragement and comfort.
> Here is the truth I flee from in my own body—
> the cosmic wit of each cell's purulescence:
> this stench of death and urine, this bulging pubes
> flecked with matted hair.
> Here are your gates of eternity, your pit, your trapdoor,
> your fissure in the earth before which the priestess sways.
> Here is the lair of tabu, the grove of ritual.
> Here I was born.
>
> I am up to my elbows in filth,
> inescapably undead.
> There is no cleansing from this.
> There is only rage, and the instinct older than love
> that thrusts my arms in deeper,
> grasping the life that is her, is myself,
> the spirit raining pus for iridescence,

the infection of being alive
which I shall never again disclaim.[16]

Morgan's "return to the body" redeems the body for her. This
redemption is experienced, through poetic imagery, as a vision,
a "cosmic" imagining. The "Network of the Imaginary Mother"
is exactly that: a network of images, beautifully constructed,
whereby Morgan explores and celebrates life by touching, "what
it is like, this being alive." Her apotheosis is a celebration of
herself:

140

> Witch-queen, sorceress,
> I must live within this body, my final home—
> here to decode each runic fingerprint,
> to trust the assurance of each hair's whitening,
> to recognize the clue left by each stretch-mark.
> My taste is salty, my smell ammonial.
> My knuckles can crack like willow-bark
> and hairblades cover my hide
> stubborn as fine grass.
> My nails are crisp as relics
> and every crevice—armpits, crotch,
> toe-valleys, ears, mouth, nostrils, eyes—exudes
> mucous or sweat for iridescence.
> Oh let me learn that I am beautiful to me,
> innocent as the spider—
> beyond judgment, disgust, beyond perfection—
> reconciled with her tufted claw,
> with the matted topaz of my labia.
> Let me sit at the center of myself
> and see with all my eyes,
> speak with both my mouths,
> feel with all my setae,
> know my own sharp pleasure,
> learning at last and blessedly and utterly:
> The life comes first. There is no spirit without the form.[17]

We saw, in the earlier section on the mother, how this celebration moves toward the attainment of divinity for the female
body in a stunning reversal of Catholic ritual. Thus Morgan
names the milk of the nursing mother, "the life of the world," a
"sacrament," which all must "take" and "eat" in order to live.
And she says of "menstrual blood" that it is the "eternal testament" shed "for the remission of living." There is, here, a clear
rejection of the death-blood of Christ for which humanity must
pay in guilty obedience to a harsh authority and in constant repression of the life impulses. There is also an elemental asser-

tion of the value of living-blood, the actual life-giving blood of women, guiltless and nourishing, which humanity must learn to accept and respect.

Like Rich and Johnston, Morgan's reclamation of the female body entails a transcendence of hierarchical dualism where the body (female) is inferior to the spirit (male); a transformation of the general loathing of the human body and a specific loathing of female flesh into an acceptance and celebration of first the female and then the human body; and the creation of a feminist symbolic where love represents Eros, an enrichment and encouragement of life and its creativity.

Dorothy Dinnerstein has also focused on the human body and the cultural revulsion for female flesh as part of her attempt to explain women's subordination and, beyond this, the prevalence of the death instinct in Western civilization. She follows Freud's analysis and Norman O. Brown's revisions on the theory of the predominance of Thanatos (aggression, conquest, and cruelty) as a result of repression of the body. But she locates the causes of this repression in the fact of women's exclusive child-rearing responsibility. For Dinnerstein, our fear of the flesh is displaced onto women rather than integrated into our personalities. Woman is available for this displacement (which later returns as a dirty fascination/loathing of the body of woman) because she cares for the child's body, introducing it to consciousness of both carnality and mortality. Because we as individuals cannot accept our isolation and limitations, we conveniently blame women for an unsolvable dilemma of our physical nature: that those who are born also die.

This blame takes many forms. One is the abhorrence of female flesh which is evidenced by the menstrual taboo, by men's cultural fear of being swallowed or castrated by the vagina, and by numerous mythologies which H. R. Hays, among others, has called the "myth of feminine evil." Western civilization reveals a fear and disgust for female flesh which is both well known and well documented.[18] Dinnerstein's explanation for this phenomenon is a variation on Freud and Brown with a feminist turn of mind. She says of this cultural blame and loathing of women:

> The dirty goddess is dirty not simply because the flesh that she represents is the vehicle-saboteur of our wishes, and because its meaning as hateful saboteur—split off from and thus unmodified by its meaning as lovely vehicle—makes our tie to it feel degrading. She is dirty also, more deeply dirty, for another reason: the positive side of what she em-

bodies—our old joy in the flesh and the capacity we still have
to feel the kind of contact with life that the flesh originally
carried—has been largely suppressed. The side of what she
embodies which, when it emerges, gives her real radiant goddess status—the mystic carnal truth that underlies the biblical use of the verb "to know" and makes the nude body in art
the most telling visual symbol of full human majesty—is not
only dissociated, compartmentalized; it is also in large degree denied and discounted.[19]

142

This denial results in repression of the body. But, as Freud argued, the repressed returns in a debased form. Women's degradation is part of this debasement; so too the triumph of Thanatos
over Eros. Dinnerstein continues:

> Both this failure to integrate our feelings toward the flesh and
> this debasement of what is positive in these feelings express
> our helplessness to cope with carnality, a helplessness that
> has so far permeated the death-denying, and therefore death-
> dominated, life of our enterprising species. Woman's status as
> scapegoat-idol is maintained by, and at the same time works
> to maintain, this helplessness. And what keeps her available
> for this status is her child *rearing*, not her child *bearing*,
> contribution.[20]

Woman's childrearing function, as argued earlier, allows all of
us to project our "helplessness to cope with carnality" and mortality onto the first parent. Thus the mother-bond explains good
and evil: the joys but also the limitations of the flesh; the hatred of women, including fear of the omnipotent mother, but a
great desire for women, especially for the symbiosis first experienced within the mothering relation. Dinnerstein's particular
emphasis is on women's exclusive mothering, which causes us
to associate the vulnerability of our bodies with the first person
who cares for us in an intimate fashion. She is convinced that
exclusive female care of children explains most of Western civilization's woes. Although her analysis does not account for so
much, it does at least point to the underlying causes of several
cultural phenomena: the degradation of female flesh, the emotional meaning of the link between maternity and mortality;
the reality and continuity of asymmetrical gender as a result of
asymmetrical parenting.

Dinnerstein's "return to the body," like her "return to the
mother," is an attempt to search out the sources of women's
subordination. Although she is not concerned to celebrate
openly the female body as Rich, Morgan, and Johnston do, she

does contribute to the feminist Eros by untangling the responsibility for our mortality from the responsibility for caring for us as we mature. The first responsibility should belong to each of us, individually; the second should belong equally to men and to women. We cannot integrate and accept the first responsibility, Dinnerstein argues, until we have integrated and accepted shared parenting. This means, in no uncertain terms, that men must come to care for infants, and thereby to learn both "the velvet imperative" (and its tender because perishable beauty) and the "vileness" of the same imperative. The feminist Eros is a conscious, informed love of the body and the life which it enables, although from a different perspective Dinnerstein would agree with Rich's determination that human beings need to "love with all their intelligence."

This return to the body, although poetic and theoretical, is not new to the Women's Movement. In terms of political action, the struggle for reproductive rights, especially for contraception and abortion, has been a visible example of feminist movement toward the new Eros. Efforts for stronger rape laws and for serious punishment for convicted rapists also illustrate the practical results of feminist envisioning.

However, before feminists can work toward the control of their own bodies, they have had to imagine a world where "woman hating"—sexual mutilation, "snuff" films, social violence against women—does not exist. Part of this imagining comes through the actual experience of alternatives—for example, lesbian love, women's support networks, freedom from pregnancy afforded by abortion and contraception—which lead to a heightened consciousness regarding what women's control over their own bodies would be like. Women who decide, against all odds, to fight for control over their bodies thus possess not only a sense that male control is wrong, indeed evil, but that women's control is inherently good, that is, inherently better for women, men, and society. In fighting to wrest control from men, feminists are simultaneously fighting for a different kind of world.

Because this world belongs partly to the future and partly to the present, feminist consciousness is not confined to analyses of male power (e.g., Andrea Dworkin's work on pornography, Linda Gordon's work on birth control, Mary Daly's work on sexual mutilation) but spreads outward to encompass creative imaginings of alternatives (e.g., the work of Robin Morgan,

Adrienne Rich, Cherríe Moraga and Jill Johnston, which we have just examined).[21]

These theorists are not random examples, but are representative of a broader emphasis. They focus on (1) women's sexuality—maternal, infantile, and adult—with special attention to the celebration of lesbian love as a consciously chosen alternative to heterosexual love; (2) the unique beauty and power of the female body in its reproductive and erotic capacities; (3) the politics surrounding control of women's bodies by the patriarchy and the necessity for women and men to come to terms with the body's connection to the mind in the hopes of arriving at an intelligent, life-encouraging synthesis between mind and body, form and spirit. These themes speak, in different ways, to the feminist joining of love and power in the feminist Eros.

The focus of the radical feminists I have chosen has been on the body and its beautiful and powerful potential. This focus has been criticized by a number of other feminists within the Women's Movement as biologically determinist or as asserting a teleology of the body.[22] Although I have already addressed this question in the section on du Plessis's criticism of Rich, I think it significant enough to call forth an answer in the context of my own argument.

If we return to the material source of the feminist Eros, we see that it is the forms of women's social practice which, as Marcuse predicted, set the stage for the development of a critical consciousness. I have tried to show that it is not biological mothering but the entire sphere of relational obligations which brings women closer to a protective, beneficent form of love and power that seeks to cherish life and life's continuity. Contrary, then, to the suggestion that this is a "biological" argument which cannot explain those women who *do not* feel a nurturant ethos, I believe that this is a "relational" argument which predicts some form of critical consciousness because of women's material practice: that is, their caretaking responsibility.

Woman's body as a source of meaning is understood in my argument in the context of a repressive, patriarchal culture. The feminist assertion of the beauty and power of the female body is thus made in radical opposition to the deformed representation and institutionalization of the female body under patriarchy. The "nurturant" spirit in both the "return to the mother" and the "return to the body" is not offered as a "biological" alternative to the destructive spirit of patriarchy but is posited as

144

one alternative among many others, which may or may not include other critiques based on race, culture, and class.

Adrienne Rich herself anticipated this "biological reductionist" objection when she wrote, in the afterword of her first nonfiction work, *Of Woman Born*:

> It can be dangerously simplistic to fix upon "nurturance" as a special strength of women, which need only be released into the larger society to create a new human order. . . . The "maternal" or "nurturant" spirit we want to oppose to rapism and the warrior mentality can prove a liability so long as it remains a lever by which women can be controlled through what is most generous and sensitive in us.

And Rich concludes this statement, so often overlooked by her critics, with a clear understanding of the complexity of women: "Theories of female power and female ascendancy must reckon fully with the ambiguities of our being, and with the continuum of our consciousness, the potentialities for both creative and destructive energy in each of us."[23] This is hardly the voice of a biological determinist.

But even if some feminists have erected a model of "maternal thinking" that *is* reductionist, the presence of a feminist critical consciousness manifested in the "return to the mother" and the "return to the body" is not thereby invalidated. Indeed, these twin journeys are confirmation of the source of this consciousness in women's forms of social practice: their caretaking responsibility for the body as mothers, wives, daughters, sisters, nurses, healers, and midwives, that is, as female human beings in their culturally defined roles.

Thus, far from positing some transhistorical, timeless "nurturant" ethos, I have argued that one thread of the radical feminist vision is deeply rooted in the social practice of caretaking rather than in women's biological capacity to mother. In Adrienne Rich's words, the "biological" argument fails "to recognize the full complexity and political significance of the woman's body, the full spectrum of power and powerlessness it represents, of which motherhood is simply one—though a crucial—part."[24]

Notes

1. Adrienne Rich, *The Dream of a Common Language: Poems 1974–1977* (New York: Norton, 1978), p. 48.

2. Adrienne Rich, *Of Woman Born* (New York: Norton, 1976), p. 40.

3. Ibid., p. 39.

4. Ibid., p. 284.

5. Ibid.

6. Ibid.

7. Kate Millett, *Sexual Politics* (New York: Avon, 1970), pp. 23–58.

8. Adrienne Rich, *The Dream of a Common Language*, p. 32.

9. Jill Johnston, *Lesbian Nation: The Feminist Solution* (New York: Simon and Schuster, 1973), p. 167.

10. Ibid., p. 168.

11. Ibid., p. 171.

12. Ibid., p. 181.

13. Cherríe Moraga, *Loving in the War Years: Lo Que Nunca Paso por Sus Labios* (Boston: South End Press, 1983), p. 140.

14. Robin Morgan, *Lady of the Beasts* (New York: Random House, 1976), p. 82.

15. Ibid., p. 79.

16. Ibid., p. 67.

17. Ibid., pp. 83–84.

18. H. R. Hays, *The Dangerous Sex* (New York: Putnam, 1964).

19. Dorothy Dinnerstein, *The Mermaid and the Minotaur* (New York: Harper, 1976), p. 147.

20. Ibid., p. 148.

21. See Andrea Dworkin, *Pornography: Men Possessing Women* (New York: Putnam and Sons, 1981); Mary Daly, *Gyn/Ecology* (Boston: Beacon, 1978); and Linda Gordon, *Woman's Body, Woman's Right: A Social History of Birth Control in America* (New York: Grossman Publishers, 1976).

22. See Alice Echols, "The Taming of the Id: Feminist Sexual Politics, 1968–83"; and Gayle Rubin, "Thinking Sex: Notes for a Radical Theory of the Politics of Sexuality," in *Pleasure and Danger: Exploring Female Sexuality*, ed. Carole Vance (Boston: Routledge and Kegan Paul, 1984). I am grateful to Kathy Ferguson for raising these issues in terms of my own argument.

23. Rich, *Of Woman Born*, p. 283.

24. Ibid.

146

Seven · Power—The Return to the Mother

The question of power is central to feminist theory. Because patriarchy is a system of power, of control over women's sexuality and the institutions which regulate it, one major concern in exploring the oppression of women is the nature of male power.

My argument has been that patriarchal power is anchored in the surplus-repression of the sexual understructure—those near-universal institutions of exclusive mothering, asymmetrical gender, mandatory heterosexuality and the hierarchy of male, public domains over female, private domains. This power results in a crude repression of the sexual instincts and their return as aggression and conquest in the West; the continuous social and political dominance of men; and the subordinate position of women which is maintained through pervasive violence against them.

In this context of male power, feminism can be seen as a revolt against patriarchy, against the enslavement of women for the enjoyment of men. Patriarchal power is then seen as abusive, manipulative, cruel, and inimical to the life instincts.

We have glimpsed already what feminist power might look like: nurturant, generative, transformative, generous in its protection of life; harmonious in its relationship to the natural world and in its assertion of the equality of the Self among the equality of Others. It is, above all, a *beneficent* power, the enabling side of an "active gentleness . . . with no mere will to mastery, only care for the many-lived unending forms" of life. Like the feminist form of love, this power begins in the mother-infant bond.

The association of power with mothering is common to all cultures, evidenced by goddess cults, fertility rites, and myths of generation. This association may or may not indicate the presence of matriarchy in our pre-patriarchal past, but it does reveal the tremendous force of the mother as primal power. Because, as Adrienne Rich points out, every human life is born of woman, we have all lived under the power of the mother. When feminists thus "return to the mother" in search of an alternative to patriarchy, they express "a new concern for the *possibilities* inherent in beneficent female power as a mode which is absent from the society at large."[1]

148

As in her eloquent expressions of mother-love, Rich has given depth and meaning to this beneficent power. In recovering the history of women's power, she writes, for example, that the images of the pre-patriarchal goddess cults "told women that power, awesomeness, and centrality were theirs by nature, not by privilege or miracle; the female was primary."[2] As for the male presence in earliest art, it appears "if at all, in the aspect of a child, often tiny and helpless, carried horizontally in arms, or seated in the lap of the goddess, or suckling at her breast."[3]

Citing archaeological evidence from Asia Minor, and Jungian analysis and interpretations of Great Mother worship, Rich explores the meaning for "primitive" woman of the sacred art of pottery-making. She notes, with other feminists like Elizabeth Fisher, the pivotal significance of the pot, urn, and container in the evolution of culture.[4] Given this value and the fact that pottery-making was invented by women and made taboo to men, Rich concludes:

> It does not seem unlikely that the woman potter molded, not simply vessels, but images of herself, the vessel of life, the transformer of blood into life and milk—that in so doing she was expressing, celebrating and giving concrete form to her experience as a creative being possessed of indispensable powers. Without her biological endowment the child—the future and sustainer of the tribe—could not be born; without her invention and skill the pot or vessel—the most sacred of handmade objects—would not exist.[5]

These indispensable powers were, Rich argues, *transformative*. Rather than pacific, receptive, and passive, the enclosing, encircling power of woman is generative. Thus, for Rich, it is patriarchal thinking, as in Erik Erikson's theory of woman's "inner space," which has defined woman's enveloping body and her creative potential as passive. Far from passivity, the "receptacle"—of the womb, the pot, the urn, the circle—exudes promise, activity, transformation. In pre-patriarchal times "not power *over others*, but *transforming* power was the truly significant and essential power, and this, in pre-patriarchal society, women knew for their own."[6] "Woman as transformer," then, is a manifestation of feminist power. It incorporates the biological capacity of reproduction not as confining, fearful destiny but as magical, transcendent power. Woman gives birth and nurtures, thereby creating and ensuring human life and culture. Thus, what under patriarchal conditions is seen as merely a mediating skill is viewed through the feminist eye as a unique, transformative power. Woman does not merely convert the infant into the person, she guarantees the transmission of culture, language, love, and community. Indeed, for Rich, woman's nurturing capacities enable human association and generational continuity. Women are prior to civilization, necessary for its beginnings and transmissions, even as they are deformed by its patriarchal cast.

In her recovery of pre-patriarchal images of the mother, Rich offers a wholly positive understanding of the mother and her physical and cultural powers in opposition to the masochistic yet threatening mother of institutionalized motherhood. By asserting the power of the mother as primary, Rich challenges the patriarchal law of man as higher, more conscious, more intelligent, more capable than woman. She rejects the characterization of passive woman subjugated by her carnality and fecundity. In its place she offers the symbol of woman as creator, independent and confident, integrated with and in control of her reproductive and mental powers. This historical re-vision can be seen as another means of reclaiming "rights" to the mother, to her nurturance and great capacities.

Beneficent female power is thus integrative, nurturant, and creative. It is not concerned with power over others as an extension of the Self, nor is it cruel or aggressive. It does not flinch from the necessities of protection against the "predator and the parasite" while it nourishes and enables growth. Indeed, given a violent world, such power in feminist hands would

> . . . carry out an unavoidable violence
> with such restraint with such a grasp
> of the range and limits of violence
> that violence ever after would be obsolete.[7]

Strength is the ground, the spring, of beneficence: strength of intimate knowledge, strength of purpose, strength of love. Feminist power is not weak, it is resilient. It does not posture, rage, or strive for grotesque heights from which others may be commanded. For Rich, and many like-minded feminists, this power works through the care of life itself, heeding the call to nurture yet not to sacrifice or suffer needlessly. Self-and-other creation—parthenogenesis as we have seen it expressed in Morgan, Johnston, and Daly—is the core of this power, truly a power attuned to the rhythm of the life instincts.

Rich concludes her book of poems entitled *The Dream of a Common Language* with a statement combining both themes of the feminist Eros, love and power. The book itself, in title, structure, and content, is indicative of this emphasis. The "common language" for which Rich searches is a poetry whereby women can "explode the oppressor's language" by naming "woman-to-woman relationships: mothers and daughters . . . lover and lover . . . and the spirit-sisters of a collective past and future."[8] This search, Rich argues, springs from the necessity for women to find each other, both for pure survival and for transformation of all social institutions. Beyond the meaning of the title, the division of the poems is telling. The first section is "Power," the second is "Twenty-one Love Poems," and the third is "Not Somewhere Else, but Here." In their headings, those sections promise a renaming and reformulation of power and love. The final poem, "Transcendental Etude," speaks these new names in a language both simple and familiar, drawn from women's domestic lives and from nature. When women reject patriarchy and begin to imagine and create a "common language," only then

> Vision begins to happen in such a life
> as if a woman quietly walked away
> from the argument and jargon in a room
> and sitting down in the kitchen, began turning in her lap
> bits of yarn, calico and velvet scraps,
> laying them out absently on the scrubbed boards
> in the lamplight, with small rainbow-colored shells
> sent in cotton-wool from somewhere far away,
> and skeins of milkweed from the nearest meadow—
> original domestic silk, the finest findings—
> and the darkblue petal of the petunia,
> and the dry darkbrown lace of seaweed;
> not forgotten either, the shed silver
> whisker of the cat,
> the spiral of paper-wasp-nest curling
> beside the finch's yellow feather.
> Such a composition has nothing to do with eternity,
> the striving for greatness, brilliance—
> only with the musing of a mind
> one with her body, experienced fingers quietly pushing
> dark against bright, silk against roughness,

pulling the tenets of a life together
with no mere will to mastery,
only care for the many-lived, unending
forms in which she finds herself,
becoming now the sherd of broken glass
slicing light in a corner, dangerous
to flesh, now the plentiful, soft leaf
that wrapped round the throbbing finger, soothes the
    wound;
and now the stone foundation, rockshelf further
forming underneath everything that grows.[9]

151

Like Adrienne Rich, Jill Johnston has focused on power in her "return to the mother." Her assertion that the "lesbian is woman prime" stems from her argument that girls, as boys, first loved the mother. The power and pleasure of this love is repudiated in order to fulfill the necessities of heterosexual orientation. Put another way, "rights" to the mother are given up. But lesbians, in loving women, reject men and thus male privilege. This rejection amounts to a two-step assertion of power: the power to refuse men and the power of self-choice, that is, the choice of women. By arguing the lesbian as primary, Johnston argues the primacy of mother-love over father-love, of homosexual over heterosexual preference.

Beneath this argument rests the bedrock of the mother as original creator of all life. Johnston says:

> The female was originally the self-sufficient self-recreating creature. The male one of her offspring. The male could re-create himself only through the female. Herein lies the desperation of man and culture. Or: all systems of inequity. Family, church, state, racism, despotism, feudalism, capitalism, nationalism, imperialism, communism, etc. The primary creature was parthenogenetic whether you call her a female or not. The cultural repression of woman is rooted in womb envy. If you can do it and I can't, that's *all* you can do.[10]

"Woman as parent prime" is the precursor to "lesbian as woman prime."

For Johnston, motherhood is the beginning, the source. The discovery of patrimony comes later, bringing savage restrictions like private property. Thus civilization as we have known it necessarily means the oppression of women.

> The story of civilized societies all over the world is the loss of female autonomy in some fierce struggle waged by the

man to capture the primacy of parenthood through the secondary means of culture—the ownership of the instruments of (re)production in his own name and through the legal apparatus for inheritance.[11]

Power over the mother and all women comes with the confinement of female sexuality in both erotic and reproductive aspects. The mother is given, transferred to the father; women become the exchange value of society.

In this situation, Johnston argues, women need radical solutions. First, they need to withdraw from men, repudiating male control and prerogative—separatism. Then women need to band together, to experience psychic parthenogenesis individually and collectively. This means an assertion of purely female power —sisterhood. Finally, women need to realize their tremendous potential to gratify each other—lesbianism. In this three-part evolutionary process, Johnston has *rejected* the control and use of women's power by men, *taken back* the power of self-creation for women, and *asserted* the right of women to love each other, completely controlling their own sexual preference. Here, feminist power is the courage of self-assertion, the struggle for an alternative, and the strength to live one's passion. Nurturance is both for one's self and for the community of women; generation focuses on an alternative society—sisterhood; transformation occurs in the move from social oppression and sexual repression to political and sexual liberation.

Clearly, sisterhood emerges as the major force of feminist power in these analyses. Johnston and Daly focus on the lesbian journey, Rich on an expansion of consciousness, the naming of an entirely other and feminist world. But the common ground is a collective of women experiencing a sense of solidarity, sharing their life concerns and committed to an alternative mode of being and living. This alternative has broad implications: a transformation of the basic sexual institutions of society through a release and refashioning of the life instincts. In the lesbian vision, we can glimpse the breaking of surplus-repression: a recovery of female power as parent prime and thus a rejection of parenting and exclusive gender categories under patriarchal conditions; an assertion of sexual choice and the nature of that choice as lesbian, resulting in a rejection of mandatory heterosexuality and of the right of men to control and exchange women's erotic/reproductive capacities. The challenge to male authority and thus to patriarchal civilization is clear. The feminist "return to the mother" moves from a remembering of the mother bond to a naming and acknowledging of this bond as primary to an articulated yearning for mother love to a political/personal commitment to women.

Mary Daly, like Rich and Johnston, has also given substance to the power of women in her imaginative leap into a feminist future where the fire of female friendship burns out the roots of gynocidal patriarchy. Daly's description of sisterhood is both moving and revealing.

153

> Far from being opposites, then, sisterhood and female friendship are not clearly distinct. A feminist thinks of her close friends as sisters, but she knows that she has many sisters— women extremely close in their temperaments, vision, commitment—whom she has never met. Sometimes she meets such women and some conversation unmasks the similarities between them. She may have an uncanny feeling that she has known these women for years, that the present conversation is merely one in a series of many with these women. The proximity that she feels is not merely geographic/spatial. It is psychic, spiritual, in the realm of inner lifetime. She senses gynaesthetically that there is a convergence of personal histories, of wave-lengths. She knows that there is a network of communication present, and that on some level, at least potentially, it exists among women who have never met or heard of each other. Because of limitations of energy, time, space, these women are not actually her friends, but they are sisters, potential friends.[12]

The power of sisterhood rests in a shared vision, not merely in a common, although fierce, dislike of patriarchy. And this vision, Daly notes, is the refusal of self-sacrifice, the courage of self-creation, and the creation of female bonding. The nature of this bonding and the many pitfalls inherent in its attainment require, Daly says, that women must be on their guard against internal patriarchal habits and external patriarchal politics. What enables women to survive and grow is sisterhood, the actual reality of other women embarking on a similar journey.

Daly's imaginative symbolic itself can be seen as a claiming of feminist power. She has renamed whole areas of patriarchal ideology while constructing a new medium through which feminists can speak to each other. Like Rich, she seeks to explode the oppressor's language.

In Cherríe Moraga's poem "What Is Left," which we examined earlier, there is a clear sense of power in the "return to the mother." Part of this power comes from the demands of Moraga's struggle as a Chicana lesbian. There is a strength of character and of vision that develops out of such a struggle. There is also the kind of power that is life-enhancing and liberatory because it is based in mother-love, the love that nurtures and encourages life. Moraga first describes such power when it is deformed and repressed:

154

> Mama
> I use you
> like the belt
> pressed inside your grip
> seething for contact.

She then notes the effects of this repressed power on her:

> the damage
> has defined me
> as the space you provide
> for me in your bed.

And finally, Moraga ends by asserting the power of resistance in the name, and for the purpose of mother-love, and of its conscious extension as lesbian love:

> I was not to raise an arm against you
> But today
> I promise you
> I *will* fight back
> Strip the belt from your hands
> and take you
> into
> my arms.[13]

In Dorothy Dinnerstein's "return to the mother," power is also a crucial concern, but not in the same fashion or with the same purpose as Rich, Johnston, and Moraga. Dinnerstein argues that it is the fear of female power which explains the existence of male dominion and women's willing subordination to it. This elemental fear is the result of our absolute dependency on the mother during a long and impressionable infancy. This dependency, in turn, is the result of women's exclusive responsibility for the care of children. Dinnerstein's logic is without the benefit of Rich's reclaiming of women's history, indeed, without the benefit of much of feminist work on women's ignored or maligned past. For Dinnerstein, the argument is still "too much mothering" rather than, in Rich's phrase, "too little fathering." Thus Dinnerstein states:

> *The crucial psychological fact is that all of us, female as well as male, fear the will of woman.* Man's dominion over what we think of as the world rests on a terror that we all feel: the terror of sinking back wholly into the helplessness of infancy.
>
> *Female will is embedded in female power, which is under present conditions the earliest and profoundest prototype of absolute power.*
>
> *Power of this kind, concentrated in one sex and exerted at the outset over both, is far too potent and dangerous a force to be allowed free sway in adult life. To contain it, to keep it under control and harness it to chosen purposes, is a vital need, a vital task, for every mother-raised human.*[14]

The escape from the mother, Dinnerstein goes on, explains the refuge in the father; or, male authority is more appealing than female authority. Male authority has been bad, indeed, it has led civilization into destruction and tyranny, but it has enabled all of us to cope with our inability to be responsible for ourselves, to be *both* nurturant and independent. The mother, while she has helped us to maturity, has also implanted within us a tremendous fear of female will. For Dinnerstein, this fear is so deep and strong that it overrides other, healthier feelings, like love and attachment which we also learn first in the mother-infant bond. Thus Dinnerstein concludes:

> Male rule of the world . . . has its emotional roots in female rule of early childhood. Man's private ascendancy in his relations with woman, and his public prerogative to represent the common adult will, serve inexorable needs for mother-raised humans of both sexes. Male rule is, to be sure, wasteful, overburdening as it does the willful-executive resources of man and the empathic-nurturant resources of woman. It is, to be sure, a vehicle of communal self-betrayal, appeasing as it does our impulse to overthrow tyranny while allowing us to go on dodging freedom's challenge. It does, to be sure, constrict and deform us as individuals, and allow us as a species to put off the awareness of communal self-responsibility that could still save us. Nevertheless, *male rule has embodied an essential human effort, an effort to cope with the emotional problems posed by our long infancy.*[15]

Dinnerstein's argument is made from a Freudian background, where psychological needs are overweighted in terms of understanding human behavior. She seems unaware of the long history of men's violent crimes against women, or she refers to these crimes in general terms as merely a buttress to an internalized psychological need for male domination. Women's beneficent, transformative power as creator and as transmitter of culture appears nowhere in her analysis. Neither does she credit women with any meaningful contributions to history. Moreover, in her analysis of the sexual relations between men and women, Dinnerstein refers to women's erotic capacities in sexist, disparaging terms that reveal both an ignorance of female erotic capacity and a heterosexual bias. For example, Dinnerstein refers to woman's clitoris as "superfluous";[16] she describes women's sexual pleasure in intercourse as "masochistic";[17] and she argues, incredibly, given recent writings to the contrary, that women *willingly* sacrifice sexual pleasure in intercourse out of guilt for their desertion of the mother.[18]

This desertion is seen through other feminist eyes like those of Morgan and Rich, as the "theft" of the mother by patriarchy. It is the sexual understructure which ensures and commands heterosexual orientations, not women's willing desertion of the mother because of their innate heterosexuality. Indeed, Dinnerstein's own male mentors, Freud and Norman O. Brown, understand this theft and the resulting struggle between fathers and brothers better than Dinnerstein does. Both men assumed a polymorphous bisexuality in the human which is forced into a heterosexual mode by the demands of reproduction and (patriarchal) civilization. Dinnerstein, however, assumes basic heterosexual orientation even while she acknowledges that all children are first matrisexual.

Beyond her confusion regarding human sexuality, and her bias toward heterosexuality, Dinnerstein's critique of male power as simply a refuge from female power ignores both the terribly cruel aspects of male power (is fascism explainable primarily in terms of an escape from the mother?) and the gentle, loving aspects of female power. Unfortunately, many feminists have accepted Dinnerstein's analysis here without critical examination.

Nancy Chodorow has also considered the question of power in her psychoanalytic study of the reproduction of mothering. Like Dinnerstein, she has argued against women's exclusive mothering, but without Dinnerstein's sweeping and inaccurate historical generalizations. Chodorow's specific contribution has been her linking of women's mothering with a large disparity in relational capacities between girls and boys (greater relational capacities in girls, lesser in boys) that re-creates asymmetrical parenting. On a larger scale, however, Chodorow shows how

156

these psychological capacities and needs interlock with basic social realities—public over private realms, the split between "life" and "work"—to ensure the domination of men. Her concern with the issue of power is a concern with women's powerlessness relative to men. This powerlessness has its roots in the sexual division of labor, specifically in women's mothering. For women to change their unequal relationship to men, therefore, early care of children must be equally shared between men and women. Put another way, the linchpin of the sexual understructure must be altered or women will remain less powerful than men.

Chodorow does not argue, as Rich and Morgan do, for example, for a special kind of feminist power. Of course, she may support the future reality of a power which is beneficent. Given her hope for egalitarian child care, Chodorow probably shares the overall feminist concern about transforming aggressive patriarchal power. But her work is focused on a clear accounting of how the sexual division of labor is reproduced in a way that ensures the domination of men and the restriction of most women to mothering and other relational/nurturant tasks. In this manner she has contributed to an understanding of why women lack power and how they can begin to assert power over their own lives.

Robin Morgan's contribution to a beneficent, transformative power is most clearly enunciated in the same poem examined in previous sections, "The Network of the Imaginary Mother." We have already seen her assertion of woman's power in her segment on the Self where themes of radical self-affirmation are expressed as a litany of love for her own body (brain, breast, womb). This recovery of the female body is also a reclamation of power. Remembering Morgan's analysis of women's internal colonization, we have a context in which to understand her praises of the Self and all women. The first stage of revolt in the colonized is a taking back of the Self from the confining realm of the colonizer. Women's self-definition, then, is at once a usurpation of patriarchy's right to define women and at the same time a statement of legitimacy against this definition.

In other segments of the poem, Morgan speaks to a nurturant feminist power which, beyond self-creation, protects life and the living. For example, she writes of the mother's abiding power to shape the child and the adult despite the deformations of an aggressive, acquisitive world. Speaking to her son in the section entitled "The Child," Morgan says:

But you have come five-fold years
and what I know now is nothing
can abduct you fully from the land where you were born.
I am come into my power, oh littlest love,
fruit of my flowering. . . .[19]

158   This beneficent power, Morgan envisions, will strive mightily
to create a world wholly different from the "kingdom of the
fathers."

I say:
you shall be a child of the mother
as of old, and your face will not be turned from me.
Then shall the bosom of the earth open and feed you,
rock you, safe, sleeping, on her lap.
No more will your stomachs bulge tumorous with hunger,
my children; no more will you be gaily tossed
on the soldiers' bayonet-points; no more will you scream
at the iron roar of death in the heavens;
no more will you stare through the miniature convulsion
of your newborn heroin addiction.
You shall be disinherited of all these legacies.
And in their place,
and in your footprints,
tendrils green with possibility will tremble
awake.[20]

Note Morgan's use of nature ("tendrils," "green") as a metaphor
of the child's growth and potential. Here, nature is not viewed
as a lesser, hostile realm in need of subjugation to the realm of
culture. Rather, nature is seen as a prototype for harmonious
growth and balance. Thus has Morgan asserted feminist power
by reclaiming a symbiotic relationship between nature and
humanity.

Balance as an expression of feminist power and a repudiation
of patriarchy's *power over* also appears in Morgan's vision of sisterhood, a collective of women and women's power. She says
that mother and daughter, as well as sister and sister, can be

a balance of sisters who appear equals of each other
and of the task as well. . . .[21]

Such equality grows from mutual nurturance, a reciprocity of
love which enables self and other creation.

Morgan is deeply conscious of weaving her eloquent argument in opposition to patriarchal institutions and ideology.
When she writes of equality and balance, it is with a heightened

awareness of the destructive absence, indeed, negation of these very qualities in our society. This explains Morgan's repetition of two basic themes throughout the twenty-five pages of the poem: "The life comes first. There is no spirit without the form," and "I disown none of my transformations. I affirm all of my transformations."

As I have argued, the first theme speaks to the necessary joining of mind/intellect/spirit with body/sensuality/desire in a mindful harmony which protects and enriches life. The other theme speaks to an assertion of the female Self as powerful, generative, and transformative. Love becomes a wise posture toward life, rather as Marcuse has argued. Power becomes the enabling care and expression of life. Both love and power resurrect and refashion Eros against a Thanatos based on severe sexual repression, negation of the body, and a resulting cruelty of power over nature and people.

Finally, the feminist emphasis on love and power attains distilled articulation in Audre Lorde's suggestive article "Uses of the Erotic: The Erotic as Power." In the title alone, we can see the synthesis of love and power into the erotic, which Lorde defines as "an assertion of the lifeforce of women."[22] Here, Eros is recalled in its classical and psychoanalytic meaning as *life instinct*. There is also an indication of this life instinct as a power unto itself. Finally, there is the explicit statement that this power has creative uses.

For Lorde, the erotic has been both denied and deformed, particularly in women. As the life force, however, the erotic is "a resource within each of us that lies in a deeply female and spiritual plane, firmly rooted in the power of our unexpressed or unrecognized feeling."[23] This resource, because it has been abused and devalued, has been used to oppress women.

> On one hand the superficially erotic has been encouraged as a sign of female inferiority—on the other hand women have been made to suffer and to feel both contemptible and suspect by virtue of its existence.
>
> It is a short step from there to the false belief that only by the suppression of the erotic within our lives and consciousness can women be truly strong. But that strength is illusory, for it is fashioned within the context of male models of power.[24]

For women who trust to their innermost feelings, their body-and-mind senses working in conjunction, the erotic "offers a well of replenishing and provocative force to the woman who does not fear its revelation, nor succumb to the belief that sensation is enough."[25]

For Lorde, the erotic is a wellspring of inspiration. It is an inner voice which speaks to us through our senses: of what is healthy, sincere, and life-enriching. It is not merely our sexual desire, but an entire sensuality, which connects the various capacities of our sentient selves and which moves this harmonious whole toward excellence. Lorde gives voice to the feminist impulse toward courageous living and thinking. As a Black poet, she expresses a striving toward unity and synthesis in her "work" and her "life." Thus she says:

> The erotic is not a question only of what we do. It is a question of how acutely and fully we can feel in the doing. For once we know the extent to which we are capable of feeling that sense of satisfaction and fullness and completion, we can then observe which of our various life endeavours bring us closest to that fullness.
>
> The aim of each thing which we do is to make our lives and the lives of our children more possible and more rich. Within the celebration of the erotic in all our endeavours, my work becomes a conscious decision—a longed-for bed which I enter gratefully and from which I rise up empowered.[26]

The "conscious decision" here refers to the control of one's life, to the "possibility" for growth and balance which Morgan seeks to give her child. It means, for Lorde, the power to "examine the ways in which our world can be truly different." One of these ways is the assertion of the erotic, "that creative energy empowered, the knowledge and use of which we are now reclaiming in our language, our history, our dancing, our loving, our work, our lives."[27]

Like Morgan, Lorde is very conscious of the feminist awakening and is one of its more articulate contributors. Much of her concern is focused on redefining women's capacities. The erotic is transformed in her work from the familiar patriarchal sexual definition to something much larger, more encompassing, and enriching. The erotic becomes "the *nurturer* . . . of all our deepest knowledge"; it functions as an equalizer between different people, constructing a bridge across which a deep sharing of the physical, emotional, spiritual and intellectual expressions may occur. This sharing, characteristic of the feminist Eros, is another manifestation of beneficent, transformative power. It stands in clear, challenging opposition to the patriarchal logos of domination which defends the appropriation of Others as extensions of the Self. In Lorde's formulation, there is an assumption of two Selves in reciprocal relation to each other. There is no hierarchy, no acquisitive, predatory relationship here.

The erotic enables the surfacing and connecting of our deepest needs while it also allows a basis for sharing with others. In this respect, the erotic is a response to alienation, to the patriarchal separation of mind from body, "life" from "work," love from power. Knowledge of our erotic selves, therefore, is itself an empowering. Lorde argues,

> When we begin to live . . . in touch with the power of the erotic within ourselves, and allowing that power to inform and illuminate our actions upon the world around us, then we begin to be responsible to ourselves in the deepest sense. For as we begin to recognize our deepest feelings, we begin to give up, of necessity, being satisfied with suffering, and self-negation, and with the numbness which so often seems like their only alternative in our society. Our acts against oppression become integral with self, motivated and empowered from within.[28]

Connected to our erotic life force, we are in a position of strength. We can rebuild relationships and whole societies because we have rebuilt ourselves, returned to an inner source of strength. The consequence of this reconnected strength is a repudiation of slave status, of definition by the colonizer. "In touch with the erotic, I become less willing to accept powerlessness, or those other supplied states of being which are not native to me, such as resignation, despair, self-effacement, depression, self-denial."[29]

Marcuse's critique of women's "relational subjectivity" as holding revolutionary potential is here creatively stated. Women's strength of lifeforce empowers them, and by so doing makes powerlessness—the essential condition of female subjugation—intolerable. Rephrased: women's reclamation of Eros leads to self-definition and self-assertion which, in turn, leads to a struggle against oppression, a taking back of power from the patriarchy. Lorde concludes:

> Recognizing the power of the erotic within our lives can give us the energy to pursue genuine change within our world,

rather than merely settling for a shift of characters in the same weary drama.

> For not only do we touch our most profoundly creative source, but we do that which is female and self-affirming in the face of a racist, patriarchal, and anti-erotic society.[30]

162 In the "return to the mother," feminist power has revealed itself as:

1. Reclamatory—a *taking back* of women's history, particularly the role of the mother and her powers of generation and transformation which women need to experience as uniquely theirs rather than as exchangeable commodities between and among men. This *taking back* entails a re-visioning of women and of history, and a celebration of what is uniquely female and powerful.

2. Self-assertive—a strong commitment to women's self-definition apart from and against traditional patriarchal definitions. This assertion is part of the generative and transformative power of the feminist Eros.

3. Integrative—a posture which continuously seeks to balance the human and the natural, the natural and the cultural, the intellectual and the spiritual, the political and the analytical. This integrative, synthesizing impulse arises in opposition to the splintering, divisive *power over* attitude of the patriarchal Self.

4. Collective—a practicing sisterhood, refusing patriarchal collectivities based on the dominating Self. The emphasis is on an equality among Selves, a sisterhood joined in pursuit of expression and creation but with special attention to nurturance and care.

5. Beneficent—an encompassing characteristic unifying all other aspects of feminist power, and which has as its purpose the power of continuing, protecting, and enriching life and the life instincts. In the largest sense, this quality opposes the patriarchal Thanatos of aggression, cruelty, and destruction.

Notes

1. Adrienne Rich, *Of Woman Born* (New York: Norton, 1976), p. 73.

2. Ibid., p. 94.

3. Ibid.

4. Elizabeth Fisher, *Woman's Creation* (New York: Anchor Press/Doubleday, 1979).

5. Rich, *Of Woman Born*, p. 97.

6. Ibid., p. 99.

7. Adrienne Rich, *The Dream of a Common Language* (New York: Norton, 1978), p. 28.

8. Ibid., back cover.

9. Ibid., pp. 76–77.

10. Jill Johnston, *Lesbian Nation: The Feminist Solution* (New York: Simon and Schuster, 1973), p. 187.

11. Ibid., p. 251.

12. Mary Daly, *Gyn/Ecology: The Metaethics of Radical Feminism* (Boston: Beacon, 1978), p. 371.

13. From *Pleasure and Danger*, ed. Carole Vance (Boston: Routledge and Kegan Paul, 1984), p. 419.

14. Dorothy Dinnerstein, *The Mermaid and the Minotaur* (New York: Harper, 1976), p. 161, Emphasis in the original.

15. Ibid., p. 200, Emphasis in the original.

16. Ibid., p. 150.

17. Ibid., p. 133.

18. Ibid., pp. 64–65.

19. Robin Morgan, *Lady of the Beasts* (New York: Random House, 1976), p. 81.

20. Ibid., pp. 81–82.

21. Ibid., p. 76.

22. Audre Lorde, "Uses of the Erotic: The Erotic as Power" in *Sister Outsider* (New York: The Crossing Press, 1984), p. 55.

23. Ibid., p. 53.

24. Ibid.

25. Ibid., p. 54.

26. Ibid., pp. 54–55.

27. Ibid., p. 55.

28. Ibid., p. 58.

29. Ibid.

30. Ibid., p. 59.

Eight · Power—The Return to the Body

Like feminist love, feminist power has meant a reclaiming of woman's body from the ideology and institution of patriarchy. In asserting their claims to control and enjoy their bodies, feminists have had to fight an internal struggle against a colonizing ideology which has defined women in physical terms for the benefit of men. The struggle is akin to the Black struggle for identity in this one respect: both women and Blacks are subjugated by a dominant ideology which, once internalized, becomes the voice of authority. Thus Blacks, as Fanon explained, must fight and overcome an internal yearning to be White. For women, the struggle is pitted against a gender identity which is grounded in institutional motherhood. Thus women must overcome a deformed identity as merely breeder/feeders before they can begin to explore and accept their bodies and exclusive control over them. This struggle has caused profound confusion and deep-rooted agony in many women because a "return to the body" is seen as but another attempt to confine women to erotic/reproductive definitions. Adrienne Rich has commented on this tension, noting that the Nature/Culture division threatens to divert feminists from their rightful attempt to join and integrate the wisdom of the body with the wisdom of the mind.

> We have tended either to *become* our bodies—blindly, slavishly, in obedience to male theories about us—or to try to exist in spite of them. . . . Many women see any appeal to the physical as a denial of mind. We have been perceived for too many centuries as pure Nature, exploited and raped like the earth and the solar system; small wonder if we now long to become Culture: pure spirit, mind. Yet it is precisely this culture and its political institutions which have split us off from itself. In so doing, it has also split itself off from life, becoming the death-culture of quantification, abstraction, and the will to power which has reached its most refined destructiveness in this century. It is this culture and politics of

abstraction which women are talking of changing, of bringing to accountability in human terms.[1]

The change to which Rich refers begins with women's unique, indeed privileged, perspective on their own oppression. I have argued that this perspective derives from women's relational qualities, those capacities and needs that Chodorow has identified as the psychological result of exclusive female child care. In suffering their colonized conditions, women have come to understand the causes of their oppression. Feminists are, in this respect, the articulate voice of the oppressed, that is, of women. But more than this, feminists bring a different and radical consciousness to the fore. Part of this consciousness is a critical appraisal and renaming of women's history. Another part is a serious analysis of patriarchy and its intimate workings. Still another component of this radical consciousness is what I have called the feminist Eros, a vision of a future feminist world where love and power, redefined, are the basis of a healthful, nurturant society. Through the feminist eye, Eros comes to triumph over Thanatos, releasing the life instincts from the bondage of the sexual understructure.

We have seen, many times, how feminists like Rich, Moraga, Morgan, and Johnston, have attempted to reclaim their bodies, to touch, in Rich's words, "the unity and resonance of our physicality." This reclamation includes, for example, a new perspective on menstruation and the menstrual taboo—one of patriarchy's most pervasive and most insidious forms of power over women's minds and bodies. Rich suggests, as part of her uncovering of women's hidden history, that we begin to think of the menstrual taboo in its positive aspects, that is, as a time for women to touch an inner core within themselves, to reflect and gain insight into the mysteries of the body. Perhaps, she argues, women themselves instituted the taboo as a form of self-segregation to enable a period of reflection. It is possible, then, that the subsequent history of the taboo as a confinement of women due to defilement was really a response by men to women's attempts to be separate and alone. If patriarchy has taught anything, it is that women lacking the control of men are threatening. Rich argues: "I would suggest that if women first created a menstrual taboo, whether from a sense of their own sacred mysteries or out of a need to control and socialize the male, this taboo itself must have added to their apparent powers, investing them with the charisma of ritual."[2]

166

This positive attitude toward the menses has also been seen in Robin Morgan's poem "The Network of the Imaginary Mother," where, we recall, she refers to menstrual blood as the "eternal testament,"

> This cup, this chalice, this primordial cauldron
> of real menstrual blood
> the color of clay warm with promise,
> rhythmic, cyclical, fit for lining the uterus
> and shed for many,
> for the remission of living.[3]

The reclamation of women's bodies is also seen in the celebration of the female genitals (which we have noted in previous sections) as beautiful, erotic, life-giving, autonomous, and unique. Morgan says to herself, and to all women, "let me learn that I am beautiful to me."[4]

Beyond this kind of intimate celebration, there is also a growing feminist consciousness about women's tremendous capacity for sensual and sexual enjoyment without men. For example, Jill Johnston's polemical statement against Freud is based on women's capacity for sexual pleasure independent of men: "I take issue like the feminists with Freud's postulation of 'heterosexual maturity.' Since a woman can achieve vaginal orgasm herself or with another woman clearly his case for maturity was in the interests of the continuation of phallic imperialism."[5]

The deep sensual satisfactions of maternal sexuality are also a part of women's independent capacity to achieve physical gratification. As such, they have been duly noted and celebrated. Morgan and Rich, among others, have begun to speak of the pleasures of nursing and of orgasm from continuous stimulation of the nipple during nursing. The contemporary focus on different kinds of birthing techniques also stresses sensual contact and bonding between mother and infant. Indeed, connections are repeatedly drawn between stages of labor and stages of orgasm, focusing on engorgement of the pelvis and the experience of bearing down. From a scientific point of view, this has been expressed by Masters and Johnson as

> the sensation of clitoral-pelvic awareness . . . described by a number of women as occurring concomitantly with a sense of bearing down or expelling.
>
> Twelve women, all of whom have delivered babies on at least one occasion without anesthesia or analgesia, reported

that during the second stage of labor they experienced a grossly intensified version of the sensations identified with this first stage of subjective progression through orgasm.[6]

From a poetic point of view, this same identification has been described in terms of feminist power. Writes poet Sue Silvermarie:

> I find now, instead of a contradiction between lesbian and mother, there is an overlapping. What is the same between my lover and me, my mother and me, and my son and me is the motherbond—primitive, all-encompassing, and paramount.
>
> In loving another woman I discovered the deep urge to both be a mother to and find a mother in my lover. At first I feared the discovery. Everything around me told me it was evil. Popular Freudianism cursed it as a fixation, a sign of immaturity. But gradually I came to have faith in my own needs and desires. . . . Now, I treasure and trust the drama between two loving women, in which each can become mother and each become child.
>
> It is most clear during lovemaking. . . . When I kiss and stroke and enter my lover, I am also a child re-entering my mother. I want to return to the womb-state of harmony, and also to the ancient world. I enter my lover but it is she in her orgasm who returns. I see on her face for a long moment the unconscious bliss that an infant carries the memory of behind its shut eyes. Then when it is she who makes love to me . . . the intensity is also a pushing out, a borning! She comes in and is then identified with the ecstasy that is born. . . . So I too return to the mystery of my mother, and of the world as it must have been when the motherbond was exalted.
>
> Now I am ready to go back and understand the one whose body actually carried me. Now I can begin to learn about her, forgive her for the rejection I felt, yearn for her, ache for her. I could never want her until I myself had been wanted. By a woman. Now I know what it is to feel exposed as a newborn, to be pared down to my innocence. To lie with a woman and give her the power of my utter fragility. To have that power be cherished. Now that I know, I can return to her who could not cherish me as I needed. I can return without blame, and I can hope that she is ready for me.[7]

Silvermarie has linked the feminist "return to the mother" and the "return to the body." In speaking of love, she also speaks of power, and both are traced back to the mother-bond, where love and power are first experienced. We also see the transformative and beneficent aspects of feminist power as expressions of intimate love and care. The relation is an equal one. The Self is expanded, but not at the cost of another. There is no annihilation of the Self as there is in sentimentalized, romantic heterosexual love and in institutional motherhood. Rather, the passage conveys a sense of rebirth through a "return to the mother." This rebirth is available to both lovers: merging with the loved one is experienced by both, not only by one and vicariously by the other, as appears so often to be the case in heterosexual relationships.

Beyond this, the "power" in this kind of lovemaking is characterized as *fragile*, and the response as *cherishing*. Both terms illustrate the nurturant, caring, tender emphasis in the feminist Eros. It is instructive to note that Shere Hite's survey of sexual attitudes and practices in middle-class women across the United States reveals that much of the strain in heterosexual relationships stems from an emotional incongruity (as Chodorow might have predicted) which is experienced in lovemaking as a lack of tenderness and concern for the woman's emotional and physical gratification. Tellingly, the section on lesbianism in Hite's survey supports Silvermarie's description of identification and symbiosis with the loved one and reciprocity regarding gratification. At least for middle-class women, it appears that heterosexual lovemaking and the sexual embrace are often alienating, frustrating experiences—as opposed to lesbian experiences, which seem, at first description, more tender and gratifying.

Along with the reclamatory and exploratory aspects of the feminist "return to the body" has come an assertion of women's sexual passion in heterosexual, not only lesbian, relationships. Against a historical, patriarchal characterization of women as "passionless" (a legacy from the Victorian period),[8] twentieth-century American mores have seemed to become increasingly liberal. Women are expected to feel sexual desire, to partake of sexual experience within marriage and outside marriage, and to seek physical if not emotional gratification in these experiences. Of course, part of this liberalization has meant tremendous pressure on men to acknowledge *and gratify* female desire. Many men find this egalitarian consideration of women's sexuality both frightening and offensive. As we have seen, women asserting themselves pose a threat to male control and authority.

But women challenging their status as sexual servants of men doubles both the threat and the offense, for the sexual under-structure is directly attacked by women's attempt to control their own sexuality. It is little wonder that many men find an awakening sexual awareness in women a fearful prospect.

Part of this awareness and the male reaction to it can be seen in the *Three Marias: New Portuguese Letters.*[9] As an exploration, through poetry and analysis, of the sexual subjugation of women and of women's sexual potential and right to gratification, the work is without peer. It is stunning in construction (a collective creation and interweaving of poems, letters, and political/social essays by three of Portugal's most talented writers), in its focus (the sexual covenant between men and women which has led to the use of love and passion for purposes of exploitation and control), and in its reception (the book was both banned *and* burned in Portugal, and the authors were fined and jailed for their "outrage to public decency").[10] For many feminists the book represents an eloquent, unmatched articulation of women's deepest, most intimate experiences from a politically conscious, indeed, radical feminist point of view.

For the actual three Marias who wrote the book (Maria Isabel Barreno, Maria Teresa Horta, Maria Velho Da Costa), it was an "impassioned exercise and experience of passion." Part of this exercise entailed explicit and beautiful renderings of women's overpowering sexual passion such as self-gratification.

> You call me desire: my body in search of the pleasure and the passion that deceives me: sudden, urgent, immediate desire, mounting astride passion as though to possess it completely, in a long act of love without sperm, with only my own juice.[11]

And the fullness and depth of women's eroticism when aroused by *heterosexual desire*:

> . . . Your naked feet, those feet of yours, Mariana, that are so small that they seem disproportionate to your height, as measured by the length of your naked body over which he slithers as he mounts you, inhabits you, gently bites your soft nipples, sometimes as pale as mother of pearl, some-times as deep as chestnut color as though they had stolen the tawny glint of your smooth golden hair or the curly fur of your pubis that scarcely seems a part of yourself.

> He knows precisely how to bite your mouth, your breasts; how to slip his tongue gently into the half-open crevice whose lips his fingers part, exposing it completely. The tu-

mescent fruit is erect and enfevered, juicy, heavy-scented, in
your burning uterus.

He knows precisely how to sip your mouth in little swal-
lows; his teeth rousing the cry you give, Mariana, the unre-
strained, prolonged cry that you allow to escape from your
lips: your orgasm, your spasm, your moan.[12]

But alongside this heavily sensuous description is an equally
eloquent argument against man's enslavement of woman, especially through love. The three Marias ask, again and again
throughout the book: "Will love ever find any other way save
this: love that uses or is used? Love that devours or is devoured;
that pretends to be devoured only to devour in its turn?"[13]

Under patriarchal conditions, a woman's role is "to give birth
and to remain stillborn herself";[14] to be "a companion and help-
mate . . . in other words: the eternal dependent and domestic
role in the world, coupled with the obligation to produce children."[15] And this makes of the woman a nun, for "what woman
is not a nun, sacrificed, self-sacrificing, without a life of her
own, sequestered from the world? What change has there been
in the life of women through the centuries?"[16] Man, meanwhile,

keeps building the world and digging his grave, and keeps
calling to the woman, addressing her first as "Mother," so
that she will point out to him what is good and what is evil,
and represent both for him, and take upon herself the intolerable absurdity of the established order of things. And the
man goes on building the world, with the welcoming and
productive womb of the woman as its foundation, this time
calling her "my possession, my treasure." And once having
made woman the repository of good and evil and the unbear-
able absurdity of the established order of things, it is only right
that she should now become the first victim, the guilty one.[17]

Thus inequality is built on inequality, and the connections
are made through passion, abused love, manipulation, the
"submission of the woman, then; domination of her through
passion-desire, which nonetheless bears a certain relationship to possession, to rape, even if only simulated rape."[18]
Woman, the erotic/reproductive object, is enslaved by her passion, through her passion. The result is masochism:

There is a man living with me who fights tooth and nail with
me and satisfies me in bed, and my vice (I am in love) is the
breath of life to me, to the point that I desire even the pain it

brings me, but despite this, I never allow him to lead me, to distract me, to destroy me.[19]

And again,

The aim of all my suffering
an exquisite pain
carefully inflicted upon myself.[20]

Other results are vengeance: "Vengeance is one of the uses of love and love is given us by custom and wont, for us to use."[21] And passion perverted into hurt, outrage, even murder.[22]

As all these examples imply, the genius of the *Three Marias* lies in its clear, moving, often explosive portrayal of the deformation of love and passion under patriarchal conditions of inequality and subjugation. But beyond this, there is a positive response, one which begins in sisterhood. The authors write at the beginning of their collective undertaking: "All three of us are deeply aware that we are now going beyond . . . ; we know for certain that we are leaping, hand in hand, toward depths that we have not yet created, and are still not certain we will be able to create."[23] Their creation became a unique exploration which brought the compact of love and hate between men and women, and women's sexual enslavement into the public eye and focused international attention on the bondage that is woman's life.

Out of sisterhood and the courage to write which sisterhood gave them, the three Marias were able to answer the central question of the book: "How to imagine love in a world that is all awry."[24] The love of subjugation, the passion of vengeance and masochism are decried. But what shall take the place of a love that is exploitative, manipulative, grossly and cruelly unequal? They answer, only a love where "two people love each other without either of them seeking to use or exploit the other, seeking only pleasure, the pleasure of giving and receiving. . . ."[25] And how is this love to be gained? "In bitter conflict, certainly, in exploration, but how far will it go, what new conflicts will it continue to create?"[26]

For their part, the three Marias have used their craft of writing to explore and contribute to an understanding of women's subjugation. They do not reject the possibility of reciprocal love, and they say of their effort, "Words are not a substitute for action, but they can be an aid. They can be used, for instance, to outline the political background of the problem of the woman."[27]

The kind of power to which the three Marias have given voice is the long suppressed power of women's sexuality, especially heterosexual desire. But they show how this power has been perverted by men's subjugation which leads women to be vengeful, or masochistic, and which leads men to rape and murder. The resulting sexual system, they argue, is a mutual covenant based on exploitation and abuse. In this kind of world, those who choose not to exploit will in turn be exploited. There is no other alternative. They suggest, by their tortured poetic rendering, that women must take the first step toward changing the system of sexual slavery. And with each step, they will be vilified, attacked verbally and physically, even jailed, as in the case of the three Marias themselves. By their public statement of the devastating emotional and political effects of women's subjugation, the three Marias challenged male authority at its core. The response of the Portuguese government is clear evidence of the very real threat which rebellious and creative women pose to the patriarchal system.

173

In looking at the themes of love and power in the "return to the mother" and the "return to the body," I have been guided by Marcuse's analysis and predictions. From his work and my own work, we can see how feminism manifests a form of critical consciousness rooted in women's everyday life. As a mediating agent between the memory of love and the reality of exploitation, this consciousness holds the seeds of a liberating vision. The function of this emancipatory impulse has been to challenge the repressive, deforming institutions of patriarchal society. In the case of feminist consciousness, these institutions comprise the sexual understructure. Thus, the "return to the mother" and the "return to the body" are consciously taken journeys destined to weaken the power of the sexual understructure and to make vivid the reexperiencing of instinctual gratification. In turn, these journeys enable the projection of an emancipated society: the feminist Eros.

Recently, however, the liberatory nature of this Eros has been threatened by a group of feminists who defend sadomasochism, pornography, sexual humiliation, consensual violence, and myriad other forms of domination and subjugation as a right of individual expression and as a kind of resistance, in their own way, against sexual repression.

In this criticism, what I have named the feminist Eros is characterized in derogatory terms as "soft" (meaning not rigorous in analysis), "romantic" (meaning utopian in recommendations), and historically unsophisticated (meaning that the feminist

Eros lacks a material base and epistemological justification).
Moreover, the feminist Eros is itself seen as sexually repressive.

These criticisms are inaccurate because both the material
grounding and the epistemological source of the feminist Eros
are found in women's social practice as caretakers. Further, the
presence of the feminist Eros is confirmation of its liberatory
nature; that is to say, the very fact of its opposition to patriarchal institutions and its envisioning of an alternative are evidence of the emancipatory substance of the feminist Eros.

Given a definition of Eros as the life force, the liberatory vision of the feminist Eros is focused on the expansion of Eros and
the lessening of its counterpart, Thanatos. As in other liberatory visions, however, its utopian quality contradicts the
secularized, positivist posture of modern thinking: thus the
"romantic" criticism.

But there is a more serious danger than just the plodding
complaints of positivists. The group called Samois has redefined
the life force Eros as whatever their brand of individualism dictates. Thus the defense of various sexual practices is grounded
in a typically American argument for individual expression.
Here, personal preferences masquerade as feminist theory without any material basis except, again, the assertion of individual
likes and dislikes.

Far from liberatory impulses, these defenses are actually a
distortion of the life force and its empowering potential. Domination and subordination, humiliation and aggression are supported because they are desired. There is no analysis of *why*
they are desired beyond the justification of individual preroga-
tives. That such desires may themselves constitute evidence of
the corrosive power of a dominating, aggressive society is ignored. So too, the degradation of love and desire as physical
pain, exploitation, and violence. Indeed, in the arguments of
Samois, we have proof of the predominance of a deformed Eros,
weakened and abused to the point of self-abuse.

But if Samois is a case of hyperindividualism in the service
of domination and subjugation, it is not alone on the American
landscape. Along with the celebratory violence of so much tele-
vision and film as well as hard-core pornography, Samois is
a symptom of cultural deformity. This too was predicted in
Marcuse's analysis, namely, the love of violation as the result of
the triumph of Thanatos. In the context of Marcuse's theory
and of my own argument regarding a feminist critical conscious-

ness, Samois is not a part of the liberation of Eros, but is, rather, a manifestation of its poisoning.

Notes

1. Adrienne Rich, *Of Woman Born* (New York: Norton, 1976), p. 285.

2. Ibid., p. 105.

3. Robin Morgan, *Lady of the Beasts* (New York: Random House, 1976), pp. 86–87.

4. Ibid., p. 84.

5. Jill Johnston, *Lesbian Nation: The Feminist Solution* (New York: Simon and Schuster, 1973), p. 170.

6. Quoted in ibid., p. 170.

7. Sue Silvermarie, "The Motherbond," in *Women: A Journal of Liberation*, 4, no. 1 (1974): 26–27.

8. Nancy Cott, "Passionlessness," *Signs* 4 (1978): 219–236.

9. Maria Barreno, Maria Horta, Maria Da Costa, *The Three Marias* (New York: Bantam, 1976).

10. Ibid., Introduction.

11. Ibid., p. 33.

12. Ibid., p. 121.

13. Ibid., p. 34.

14. Ibid., p. 79.

15. Ibid., p. 274.

16. Ibid., p. 154.

17. Ibid., p. 157.

18. Ibid., p. 84.

19. Ibid., p. 82.

20. Ibid., p. 43.

21. Ibid., p. 40.

22. Ibid., pp. 114–115.

23. Ibid., p. 41.

24. Ibid., p. 313.

25. Ibid., p. 89.

26. Ibid., p. 314.

27. Ibid., p. 315.

Afterword

The feminist Eros, as I have framed it, is the result of over a decade of thought and creativity by women actively engaged in their collective liberation. Utopian visions of a future without oppression, without exploitation loom large in this feminist creativity. So too insights borne of women's daily social practice.

As more women take up the speech of feminist theory, other issues will enter the discourse. For example, questions regarding the relationship of women to nature, of white women to women of color, and of Western culture to Indigenous, Black, and other non-Western cultures already inform much of the recent literature coming from the Women's Movement.

While these new dimensions deserve entire studies of their own, I would like to speculate, briefly, on their critical functions in the decade to come.

Race

Despite the contributions of Audre Lorde, Cherríe Moraga, and other women of color, the great preponderance of American feminist theory has been written by white, educated, middle-class women whose writing is informed by their class and race experiences. Beyond this, white feminists also assume a universal applicability in their analyses, and in their dreams of a future society. They argue, against the criticism that their work suffers from the limitations (and opportunities) of their life situation, that women of color have also suffered the theft of the mother, the repression and savage control of their sexuality by men, the symbolic and ideological degradation of their bodies. They too have been confined to mothering roles and the private world of the family. And they have yearned, as all oppressed peoples do, for liberation from their bondage.

But, as women of color increasingly point out, they have been exploited by white men *and* by white women. Further, this exploitation cannot be separated from sexual oppression. It is a commonplace experience in America, for instance, that women of color are preyed upon by white men who imagine them to be more animal than human, more capable of fulfilling fantasies of carnality *because* they are dark. This specific racial degradation is further compounded by white standards of beauty. Forever "failing" to be white, the woman of color is trapped by a system that finds her at once unattractive and yet alluring, at once dirty and yet fascinating. In the area of sexual images alone, then, it is clear that the sexual oppression of women of color is more complex than suggested by a simple analogy with white women's sexual oppression.

178

As members of white-dominated society, meanwhile, white feminists have also internalized racist images of women of color. In attitudinal terms, this means that women of color are seen as smutty inferiors or as dangerous exotics by white women, including white feminists. This fear and arrogance partly explains why women of color are often excluded from (or isolated within) the Women's Movement. Even when white feminists attempt to speak across the agonizing historical chasm that divides white from colored, they betray what Joel Kovel has called "aversive" racism: lip service to "ideals" of equality but an aversion to contact, to daily involvement in struggles against racism.

Nevertheless, as the most aware white feminists know, racism is a feminist issue. At least in theory, liberatory visions promise liberation for all people no matter their class, color, or culture. But beyond a general acknowledgment of racism—that is, of the systematic exploitation of people of color for the benefit of white people—there is little analysis of the interplay between white women and women of color in white feminist theory.

While thoughtful works by feminist women of color begin to appear, white feminists are increasingly challenged on both theoretical and practical political grounds. Further, what women of color have to say and how they choose to say it will set the standards for a different kind of feminist envisioning, one that white feminists will have to address. Thus, a critical function of the work of women of color will be the unmasking of American patriarchy as racist, and not merely sexist. Another critical task will be the challenge of white feminists in their universalistic assumptions.

But while women of color will no doubt continue to speak for and about themselves, their work does not remove the responsibility white feminists bear in the fight against racism. From the vantage point of the middle 1980s, it appears that in shouldering this burden white feminists must first come to a clear understanding that patriarchy in America is not just male. It is also white and racist. And beyond this, white feminists must begin to recognize that patriarchy in America is peculiarly American—that is, peculiarly egocentric, rapacious, techno-logical, profit-oriented, and destructive of the earth. White feminists have grown to maturity in this particular kind of pa-triarchy and they have learned to identify with its cultural forms, that is, with technological consciousness, urban en-vironments, capitalist markets, and instrumental relationships. Even while they are antagonistic to certain aspects of white cul-ture, white feminists embody it.

179

Therefore, they will need to turn their analyses inward to an examination of how they have been influenced by racist culture and thus harbor racist ideas and attitudes. In these times, it is simply insufficient for white feminists to protest that they are not women of color and therefore cannot understand racism. Neither is it sufficient to acknowledge a racist heritage—and then fail to move toward changing a racist society. By analogy, feminists would not allow men simply to agree that they are sexist without insisting on a change of behavior. The same, then, must hold for white feminists. The American Women's Movement is now at a critical point in its evolution. The ques-tions of race and racism cannot be pushed to the back of the theoretical or political bus any longer. White feminists can no longer flinch from the fact that in terms of privilege and power, they are to women of color as white men are to white women. And while the analogy is not exact, to women of color it has the deep feel of truth.

Beyond an initial recognition of the primacy of racism as a feminist issue, white feminists must commit themselves to an immersion in the history of people of color in America. Since white privilege depends upon ignorance, white feminists must supplant their ignorance (and its tendency to universalize white culture) with serious study of large issues such as Black slavery, the psychology of Black-White relationships, the history of the loss of Chicano lands and resources, the long and ugly tale of America's genocidal treatment of American Indians, the story of Asian peonage, and the subjugation of America's overseas colo-nies from Puerto Rico to Hawai'i and beyond.

And this is only a beginning. In learning these histories,

white feminists will begin to learn about American imperialism, and to raise questions about the link between patriarchy and global American domination. This kind of lengthy education is a litmus test for serious antiracists. In the 1980s, white feminists must move beyond their verbal opposition to racism. It is time for guilt and ignorance to be replaced by political involvement. Giving up white privilege begins with a giving up of white inaction.

180

Thus the relationship of feminist theory to racism will only be answered through joint political struggle by white women and women of color. As the material base for new critical visions, the nature of these struggles could range from Indian efforts to stop further theft of their lands and resources, Black efforts to deal with ghetto exploitation, and Chicano efforts to achieve political power, to more focused efforts to secure medical care, educational opportunities, and employment for people of color. Plainly put, it is concrete, daily experience that changes consciousness. Just as women's daily life gave rise to feminist analysis, so too should feminist activity against racism give rise to a larger consciousness about the life of people of color. What this consciousness will look like in theoretical form remains to be seen. But white feminists must turn their focus toward a different kind of consciousness-raising: alongside their explorations of male power they must now add investigations of white power.

Culture

Closely connected to the explosive issues of race are questions of culture. In America, the dominant culture is not only white, it is American. But, as with their universalizing of the experiences of white women to women of color, white feminists have universalized their understanding of culture: Indians become native Americans, Blacks become Black Americans, Asians become Asian Americans, and so on.

Surrounded by the accoutrements of urban life—bookstores, universities, theaters, factories, large institutions like hospitals and courts—white feminists have but the vaguest of notions about other cultures that have been subjugated within America. Ignorance, once again, is the prerequisite to an assumption of privilege and the continuation of cultural imperialism.

Thus white feminists need to begin to explore how they inhabit a society that is culturally, and not only racially, imperialist. They must come to understand that white culture has brought devastation and ruin to people of color around the world, not only to those Americans of color at home. This white culture has left millions dead while devouring their lands and resources for the endless consumption of white nations, particularly America. This same culture, in its dependence on technology, science, and warfare has poisoned the earth, its oceans and forests, its animals and plants, indeed, the very air we breathe. It is this culture which white feminists must disavow before they can discover paths away from "power over" people of color.

181

Of course, feminist theory in its visionary leap into a non-exploitative world hints at different, non-abusive relationships with other peoples and other cultures, indeed with the earth and its bounties. But these are only hints. They remain within the confines of white feminist experience, which is to say, within the limitations of white culture.

Since cultural imperialism—like white privilege and male power—depends upon ignorance and confusion, white feminists who would fight this imperialism and privilege must fight, before all else, their own terrible ignorance and the moral stupidity which it engenders.

Nature

Finally, the question of culture in feminist envisioning leads to the question of nature. White feminists like Susan Griffin and Carolyn Merchant have explored Western culture's approach to nature. Both have noted the characterization of nature as female and the relationship between the gross exploitation and destruction of nature and the exploitation of women and sexual violence against them. Sherry Ortner and Peggy Sanday have also tried to understand the nature/culture dichotomy and its connection to male power. While in disagreement on the precise causal relationship between the subjugation of nature and the subjugation of women, both have contributed to a larger sense that women and nature are deeply intertwined.

In terms of a critical look at feminist theory, I would say that the question of nature needs to be explored, as Sanday has explored it, within the context of other cultures. And I would offer, speculatively, American Indian cultures as a beginning.

First, Indian cultures have a dependency on and a spiritual relationship with the Earth that poses a clear alternative to white culture. To American Indians, the Earth and its creatures are not merely extensions of human sensitivity; they do not exist at the sufferance of humans, nor do they occupy an inferior position in a hierarchy where humans are at the top. The Earth, as the embodiment of Nature, precedes humans who are themselves a *part* of Nature, in no way separate and superior to it. People are but one segment in the circle of life, in the hoop of all living things. Within this circle human beings have a place alongside (not above) other living beings. This circle entails a responsibility for those within it: they must care for each other. Humans, then, have a caretaking relationship with the Earth, they are stewards of its bounties.

Western peoples, in stark contrast to American Indians, are alienated from nature because, from an Indian perspective, they have lost their soul. This soul could be said to be their "place within the natural design," a design which Western man believes is his to alter, exploit, and ultimately, destroy. Industrialization (the product of science and technology) is the means of this destruction. Thus Western peoples cannot regain their soul until they return to their place within the natural system. For several centuries, indeed thousands of years, Western people have refused their place within nature, demanding instead to stand above it. This disjunction has led to alienation from nature.

In turn, this alienation has resulted in the rapacious, exploitative West that we all know. It is only a matter of time, Indians believe, before nature rebounds on its destroyers. The poisoning of the environment is just one example. Nuclear annihilation is another.

While there is much more to American Indian relationships with nature than what I have described, this is sufficient to make my point: nature must be understood as more than a "female entity" like women, who in turn, are "like nature." No matter how useful the connection between women and nature for understanding the oppression of women, nature is beyond a simple "female" analogy. Therefore, white feminist theorists need to understand nature as a greater whole of which they are a part rather than as an extension of their nurturing capacities. Put another way, nature is only partly comprehensible through an understanding of women's oppression while more comprehensible through an harmonious existence with other living creatures.

Although this distinction may at first appear unnecessary, it is, on further thought, seen to be crucial. For just as an ignorance of people of color and their cultures allows the continuation of racism and genocide, so an ignorance of the human place within the natural design leads to an ignorance of nature itself and allows the wasteful consumption of the Earth to proceed. Even the ecological/wilderness approach remains within the view of nature as a resource for humans. The only difference between this view and the industrialists' view is that the former fights for preserves and wilderness areas. Philosophically, however, the Earth is still seen as a resource. Feminists who support this perspective, then, are part of the existing scheme. There is no spiritual substance to this approach; "eco-feminism" does not espouse the circle of life.

Central to the human place within nature is the link between consumption, profit, and survival. Clearly, humans do not need to consume at the level that industrial nations now do. Such consumption impoverishes the Third World and reinforces the warmongers' cry for larger weapons and armies. But beyond this, such consumption depletes the Earth of its living creatures while preventing the growth of a spiritual bond between humans and other forms of life. This too is an impoverishment. And it leaves a legacy of "soulless," dead people.

In their envisioning of a new world, feminist theorists have responded to this impoverishment from the particular perspective of their daily oppression. They have tried to address their specific problems of sexual dominance within the context of what appear to be other universals. While their efforts have resulted in generous, creative alternatives, they need to turn their minds to the study of other cultures, particularly indigenous cultures, to learn how to live with nature in a non-exploitative, respectful way.

Questions of race, nature, and culture are already beginning to add profound dimensions to feminist theory. The result will be even larger, more encompassing visions. In their continuing critical function and in their assertion of Utopian possibilities, these visions will continue to fulfill the promise of feminism.

186